God's Di

Understanding New Testament Divorce and Remarriage Teaching

Colin Hamer

www.apostolos-publishing.com

First Published in Great Britain in 2017

Faithbuilders, An Imprint of Apostolos Publishing Ltd,

3rd Floor, 207 Regent Street,

London W1B 3HH

www.apostolos-publishing.com

British Library Cataloguing-in-Publication Data

A catalogue record for this book is available from the British Library

ISBN: 978-1-910942-78-9

Cover Design by Blitz Media, Pontypool, Torfaen. Image: © Lasse Kristensen | Dreamstime

Printed and bound in Great Britain by Marston Book Services Limited, Oxfordshire.

More Books from Faithbuilders

The Lion and the Lamb: The Book of Revelation

Enduring Treasure: The Lasting Value of the Old Testament for Christians

Israel Restored

Hebrew Foundations of the Christian Faith

Massive Power Massive Love

Bouquet of Blesings

PLUS: The Faithbuilders Bible Study Guides

And many more…

For details of all our publications visit www.apostolos-publishing.com

Contents

Preface

This book is based on the thesis I submitted in June 2015 for the degree of Doctor of Philosophy. Although this was awarded by Chester University (UK), the study was undertaken at Union School of Theology (formerly WEST), an academic institution with a conservative evangelical tradition. It was published as *Marital Imagery in the Bible: An Exploration of Genesis 2:24 and its Significance for the Understanding of New Testament Divorce and Remarriage Teaching* (London: Apostolos, 2015).

It might be thought that nothing new could be found to say about the Bible's teaching on divorce and remarriage. But this is not so—for at least three reasons:

1.   In evangelical scholarship, it is now more fully appreciated than ever before how deeply New Testament teaching is rooted in the Old Testament, and that an Old Testament perspective should underpin our understanding of New Testament teaching.

2.   Because of an ever-expanding amount of research into biblical times, more is now known than ever before about the New Testament world—the world in which Jesus and his apostles lived.

3.   The seemingly unanimous view of those that have sought to unravel the Bible's divorce and remarriage teaching is that the model for our marriages is Adam and Eve's own marriage. But on a closer examination of the Genesis text, it can be seen that not only does Genesis not teach this, nowhere else in the Hebrew Bible (our Old Testament) teaches this either. Nor was this ever the understanding in ancient Israel, the people group to whom God gave those Scriptures.

But there is a fourth, and even more important reason to look afresh at the Bible's divorce and remarriage teaching. Previously there has only been a very limited study of Scripture's marital imagery—where God asks us to *imagine* that he is married to his people, or as it is in the New Testament, that Jesus is the bridegroom of the church. A central theme of this imagery, which runs from Genesis to Revelation, is God's own divorce and remarriage.

It will be the aim of this book to show how this significant theme should inform our understanding and teaching about the subject of divorce and remarriage in the Bible.

Various views are held by Christians on divorce and remarriage and these will be referred to as the 'traditional views.' They are a sincere attempt to accurately reconstruct the teaching of the New Testament, but as many of these views contradict each other on several key points, it is clear that these attempts have been, on the whole, unsuccessful.

I suspect that for many readers this book will present a challenge to their own, often deeply held, views on the subject. It is for that reason I want to emphasise that as a conservative evangelical I take the highest view of the Scripture as the word of God, and it is that perspective that underpinned the PhD thesis on which this book is based. To make this book as clear and accessible as possible to a wider readership, some of the detailed analysis will be kept out of the text, although the work of various scholars, and my own PhD study, will sometimes be referenced.

Acknowledgments

I have been both humbled and encouraged by the response of believers to my published PhD thesis, *Marital Imagery in the Bible*. Many—some who are at the beginning of their ministry, and others who have spent a life-time serving our Lord, some I have been privileged to count as friends, and others I have never met—have been prepared to be like the Bereans (Acts 17:11), and take a fresh look at Scripture in light of that study. The result is many more glowing commendations and published reviews than I could have ever hoped for.

As I mention in the Preface, this book is based on that PhD study. And while the views expressed in this book are my own, I would like to thank those that have given of both their time and pastoral experience to read and offer advice on Chapter 9, 'Pastoral Realties.' They include: Jeremy Bailey, Gary Brady, Rich Cozart, Peter Cranch, Eryl Davis, Hugh Davis, Tom Holland, Digby James, and Kerry Orchard. I would further like to thank Mathew Bartlett, senior editor at Apostolos, who has been a delight to work with both on this book, and my published PhD.

My interest in this subject began when I read the ground-breaking study: David Instone-Brewer, *Divorce and Remarriage in the Bible: The Social and Literary Context* (Grand Rapids, MI: Eerdmans, 2002).

After many years' reflection, and five years' full-time study, I am convinced it is one of the most (perhaps *the* most) significant works ever published in the field. Dr. Instone-Brewer was the external examiner for my PhD, and although my background is not in academia, I had an idealised concept of a scholar in my mind—remarkably erudite, and yet self-effacing. Every interaction I have had with him has demonstrated to me that he is such a man.

It would be remiss of me not to mention again Tom Holland. It was Tom, Research Supervisor at Union School of Theology (formerly WEST), who persuaded me to take the study through to a PhD, and acted as my supervisor, alongside Rich Cozart. I am immensely indebted to both men.

Finally, as I now reflect back on my life, I can see that it was Stuart Olyott's inspirational exegesis of Scripture at Belvidere Road Church each Sunday in the early 1970s that has been key to the basis of my understanding of the Bible, my subsequent Christian life—and this study.

I have stood on the shoulders of giants.

Introduction

It can only be imagined when the New Testament writers made their (albeit brief) comments on divorce and remarriage that they assumed they would be understood. So, what has gone wrong?

In the years after the destruction of Jerusalem in 70 CE, when Graeco-Roman culture was at its height, the Jewish perspective of marriage and divorce, and thus the context of those brief New Testament comments, was lost. The Christian church of that era was influenced by the neoplatonic ideas of the day, and an idealised concept of marriage developed from Adam and Eve's marriage recorded in Genesis 2:23—it was love at first sight, a marriage made in heaven. These concepts frame an understanding of marriage in much of Western culture even today.

However, that was never the understanding of ancient Israel. Instead they looked to Genesis 2:24: 'Therefore a man shall leave his father and his mother and hold fast to his wife, and they shall become one flesh'—so a naturally born man chooses a wife for himself, and their union was based on a 'covenant'—in other words an agreement. The Old Testament makes it clear what the basis of that agreement was. Furthermore, it makes clear that if the agreement was broken, there could be a divorce and a remarriage. All the Bible's marital imagery (where the both the Old and New Testament ask us to *imagine* that God is married to his people) is based on that understanding of human marriage.

But our concept of marriage is so strong that when Genesis 2:24 is referred to in the New Testament, it is thought that the reference is to Adam and Eve's marriage. It is a paradigmatic marriage that for many excludes (or greatly restricts) the possibility of divorce and remarriage.

This book looks to challenge that paradigm—and to suggest that the New Testament writers would not have employed an imagery which had at its centre divorce and remarriage, only to deny the possibility of such in their own human marriage teaching.

Chapter 1: We Believe the Bible

1.1 Scripture—the Word of God

Most evangelicals accept that the Bible was given by God as the ultimate source of knowledge about him—they believe it alone tells us how we can come to know him, and that it is our sure guide as to how we should live our lives. It not only conveys concepts which we can use to guide us in our ethical decisions, it also contains specific teaching on a wide range of issues.

But to get at the Bible's meaning it is necessary to look carefully at the actual words used, and crucially, the *context* in which they are used, to understand what it is saying. For example, in any language the same word can mean several different things, so in English we have a tin 'can,' and something you 'can' do—in this case the way the word is used in a sentence (whether as a verb or a noun) usually determines its meaning. But consider this account:

> It was a warm, sunny, late summer's evening. On the cry of 'owzat!' the captain, disconsolate, walked back to the pavilion with his bat over his shoulder.

What was it that the captain carried? A winged rodent—or a cricket bat? Here we see that it is the sentence that determines the meaning of the noun 'bat.'

Consider also this newspaper headline: 'Police say that most crime committed in the town centre on a Saturday night is caused by people drinking to excess.' Most readers will not have realised that a crucial word is missing—it is drinking *alcohol* that is being referred to. In our minds, we automatically put 'alcohol' in the sentence without thinking about it. But if we were reading that headline in a library archive in the year 2500 and alcohol was no longer available, we might struggle to make sense of it. In this example, we can see that the wider social/historical context of the account is needed to help determine what the headline meant.

The context of the words in a sentence, and the wider context of that sentence in the passage of Scripture, and the wider social context of the intended audience, are all important. The New Testament, although addressing all Christians for all ages, uses a language that a first century audience in

Palestine would understand. To understand the New Testament, we need to understand that context.

Although in the first century CE new cultural influences were flooding in from the Graeco-Roman world, day-to-day life in Palestine remained much as it had been for centuries throughout ancient Israel. Their culture was rooted in their Scriptures, the Hebrew Bible, albeit now translated into Greek. It was to that Old Testament that Jesus and the apostles repeatedly went—it formed the basis of all their teaching. E. P. Sanders says, 'There is today virtually unanimous consent … [that] Jesus lived as a Jew.'[1] And C. H. Dodd points out that Paul could argue in Acts 26:22: 'I stand here … saying nothing but what the prophets and Moses said would come to pass.'[2] G. K. Beale comments:

> there are no clear examples where they [New Testament writers] have developed a meaning from the Old Testament which is inconsistent or contradictory to some aspect of the original Old Testament intention.[3]

The repeated quotes from, and sometimes (at least for us) obscure allusions to the text of the Old Testament, demonstrate that the New Testament writers expected their readers to be very familiar with that Old Testament text.

However, it will be seen in §1.6 below, that this Jewish context was soon lost in the early post-apostolic years of the church, and an understanding of New Testament marriage teaching developed that was far removed from its original Jewish context. This in turn led to much confusion about the New Testament divorce and remarriage teaching, a confusion that has come through to our modern era.

1.2 Metaphoric Language

While accepting that the Bible is God's word, this does not mean the same as saying that everything said in the Bible is literally true. An example is found in Psalm 98:8 which says, 'Let the rivers clap their hands.' This is an example of metaphoric language—in other words, we do not think that the Bible is suggesting that a river literally has hands which it can clap. We all accept that this is what might be called 'poetic licence'—the point being made by the Psalmist is that all creation should be joyful for what the Lord has done.

However, linguists over the last fifty years or so, have pointed out that metaphors can be more than poetic licence—they can be the means of communicating knowledge, even profound truths.

The Bible uses metaphors this way a great deal. So much so that George Caird (one-time Professor of the Exegesis of Holy Scripture at Oxford University) could say that, 'All, or almost all, of the language used by the Bible to refer to God is metaphor'; he further points out that metaphors compare one thing to another and that comparison 'comprises … almost all the language of theology.'[4]

A metaphor makes this comparison by declaring that A 'is' B—even though the statement is not literally true. So, in our example from Psalm 98, a river 'is' a person, a person with hands that can be clapped. Another Old Testament example is in Psalm 23, 'the Lord is my Shepherd,' and a New Testament example is in John's Gospel when Jesus says, 'I am the door' (John 10:9)—these metaphors, when they declare that God 'is' a shepherd, and that Jesus 'is' a door—are displaying what linguists call 'false literalism.'

Thus, a metaphor helps us to understand one thing by defining it in the terms of another. In this, metaphors are like similes—if Jesus had said 'I am *like* a door'—this would be a simile. And although metaphors, like similes, compare one thing with another, Max Black suggests that something more happens to our perception when a metaphor is used:

> To think of God as love and to take the further step of identifying the two is emphatically to do something more than to *compare* them as merely being alike in certain respects. But what that 'something more' is remains tantalizingly elusive: we lack an adequate account of metaphorical thought.[5]

There is an element of mystery about how metaphors are processed by the mind that linguists are still actively exploring.

1.3   Analysing a Metaphor

Each metaphor has two parts, one is called the 'vehicle,' the other the 'tenor.' The vehicle 'carries over' characteristics (hence *metaphora* from the Greek 'to carry over') to the tenor (from the Latin *teneo* 'to hold'); thus in 'I am the door' the vehicle is the door that carries over characteristics to Jesus, the tenor, the complete statement forming the metaphor.

Although not literally true, a metaphor seeks to convey a truth, often such being left to the reader to surmise. When it is said that a metaphor is not literally true, it is not meant to say that a metaphoric statement is meaningless. Although Jesus is not *literally* a door—the statement nonetheless conveys a profound truth that transcends the function of any ordinary door. Similarly, if we say that the statement, 'Jesus is the son of God' is not to be taken *literally*, it is not meant to imply any less of Jesus's position in the Trinity, or cast doubt on his deity, it is just that the relationships within the Trinity transcend anything that human language can convey, and thus the New Testament looks to metaphors to explain them to us. These metaphors are a means of communicating something of a spiritual truth—a truth that no human language can fully express.

The metaphoric A 'is' B statement in Psalm 23:1 is that the LORD 'is' a shepherd. The 'shepherd,' is the vehicle that accomplishes the transfer to the LORD, the tenor of the metaphor. It can be seen that the vehicle has to be a known entity to achieve a meaningful transfer: thus in the metaphoric A is B, 'A' (the tenor) is often a more abstract concept that is declared to be 'B' (the vehicle), a tangible entity employed to illustrate the tenor.

In the metaphoric 'I am the door' (John 10:9), and 'this [bread] is my body' (Matthew 26:26; Luke 22:19), an ordinary door and ordinary bread are employed as vehicles to illustrate the nature of Jesus's mission and body respectively; these everyday metaphoric vehicles each illustrate a more abstract and mysterious tenor. It can often be deduced from metaphors what sort of society any intended audience lived in. For example, the New Testament speaks in its metaphors of seeds and sheep—things familiar to an agricultural society that would enable the metaphor to achieve its intended transfer from vehicle to tenor. But metaphor theory does not suggest any change in the properties of the metaphoric vehicle or tenor. In other words, seeds and sheep remain seeds and sheep, and the things they represent (the word of God and believers) do not change either—the metaphor's aim is to illustrate, to make new connections. Any change that does take place is in the reader's perception of the thing illustrated.

But metaphors, instead of clarifying meaning, can sometimes obscure it. The 'I am the door' of John 10:9 is part of an explanation following a series of metaphoric expressions about a shepherd and a sheepfold used by Jesus in a discourse with the Jews. The Gospel writer comments, 'This figure of speech Jesus used with them, but they did not understand what he was saying to them' (John 10:6). The use of additional metaphoric expressions to explain the original ones in the passage serves to underline Caird's point (noted earlier) about theological language.

Notice also Jesus's instruction to, 'Watch and beware of the leaven of the Pharisees and Sadducees' (Matthew 16:6), which from the explanation in v. 12 seems to portray the teaching of the Pharisees and Sadducees as having the potential to insidiously pervade one's mind. Here again a tangible and familiar element (how leaven permeates bread) is employed as the vehicle to illustrate a more abstract concept and heighten the disciples' awareness of it. However, the metaphor brought from the disciples the confused response: 'we brought no bread' (Matthew 16:7).

It can be seen how the understanding of a metaphor can lead to a difference of opinion for subsequent exegetes, as history demonstrates has happened with Jesus's, 'this [bread] is my body.' In any Bible exegesis, identifying a metaphor and its constituent parts is a process vital to the unravelling of the author's meaning, even if uncertainties remain.

1.4   Large Scale Metaphors

The idea in Psalm 23 that God is a shepherd of his sheep leads to several subsidiary metaphors connected with shepherds and sheep (e.g. his rod and staff comfort me). These subsidiary metaphors are called *consequent analogies*, because they are analogies that flow from the original metaphoric statement that the Lord is a shepherd. These can be diagrammatically represented like this:

MAP 1: THE LORD IS MY SHEPHERD

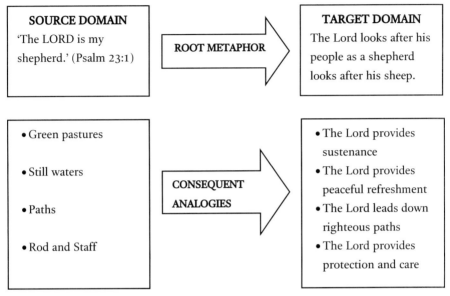

The root metaphor, the LORD IS MY SHEPHERD, is developed by Jesus in John 10 where he employs further analogies to describe his own ministry—all based on the concept of him being a shepherd. This can be diagrammatically represented like this:

MAP 2: JESUS IS THE GOOD SHEPHERD

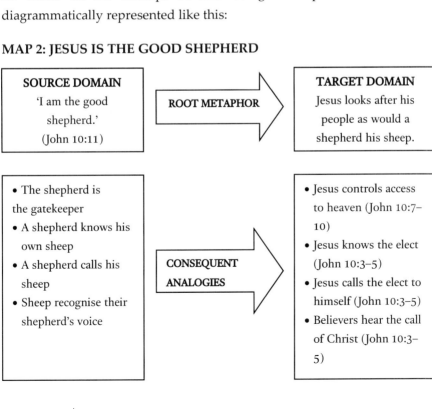

In the next chapters, it will be seen that the metaphoric statements GOD IS THE HUSBAND OF ISRAEL, and JESUS IS THE BRIDEGROOM OF THE CHURCH, are two closely related large-scale metaphors that dominate the Bible story from Genesis to Revelation.

1.5   Allusions

In addition to metaphors, we need to be aware of the possibility that a Scripture text might be referring to another Scripture text, an historical incident, or a concept. Any cross-referencing Bible demonstrates this, and there are a great many clear examples. However, as the New Testament world is being increasingly revealed by archaeologists, and by scholars specialising in the literature and documents of New Testament times, it is thought that there are other subtler allusions in Scripture that might previously have been missed by Bible exegetes. For example, it will be seen in §5.4 that when Jesus speaks of 'living water' to the woman of Samaria, it is possible that he is alluding to the ritual bath it is now known that a Jewish bride took before her wedding. If so, it seems that Jesus would be using the expression to point to the fact that he is the expected Messiah, who has come as a bridegroom to fulfil the many Old Testament prophecies of a new 'marriage.' And to offer that woman, and the people of Samaria, a place in the bridal community at his own marriage supper.

Two principal questions arise from the concept of such allusions: firstly, how valid is it to read an allusion like this into a text? And secondly, why would an author want an allusion to be implicit rather than explicit? The latter question appears to have received less scholarly attention than the former. It could be that what seems implicit to the 21st century reader was explicit to the contemporary audience. If the latter is correct then allusions might serve as a form of stylistic short-hand—bringing many things to mind with just a few words. Even though our culture today is saturated with TV, radio, cinema, books, and social media, and we are bombarded with literally millions of words and images in our lifetime, nonetheless, one phrase can cause us to recall an incident many years ago. For example, during the final seconds of the 1966 World Cup England was leading 3-2 over Germany, and as the television commentator was speaking England scored again, giving rise to his famous comment: 'they think it's all over—it is now.' I watched that football match live on television at my home as a young boy with my father and uncle. When I hear those words now, I do not just think of that match, I think of the jubilation that my father and uncle displayed, of other events that day as we celebrated, then my thoughts go to other times at my boyhood home, and of my now deceased parents—all vividly brought to mind in just a few words.

But, one might ask, why are some allusions in the New Testament so subtle that previous generations have missed them? R. T. France suggests that even if Matthew knew that not all his readers would grasp his seemingly obscure Old Testament references (in Matthew 2), he was writing in a style comparable to that of:

> many of the most successful writers of all ages, whose work has an immediate impact without extensive academic analysis, but is not exhausted on a first reading and continues to delight and reward in successive encounters over the years.[6]

As regards the first question: whether or not there really *are* subtle intended echoes and allusions in any text—despite an element of subjectivity in assessing such, it is widely thought that they can often be safely identified. Bible exegetes might look for the explicit repetition of specific words, or for the presence of stylistic or thematic patterns, and to see if the allusion fits the context—and consider the probability that the author would make such an allusion.[7]

But any such allusions are both culture and language specific. For example, when I asked my English speaking Belgian friend, what 'they think it's all over—it is now' meant to him, he looked at me blankly. Yet when I mentioned the 1966 football match he knew all about it—it is just that Belgian television had not transmitted the UK commentary.

The danger is that today we might miss some New Testament allusions that would be obvious to people living in first century Palestine. In that culture, there was no radio, television, cinema, or internet, and basically one book— the Old Testament in Greek. In the synagogue and at home that's the document they would read and be taught, and would probably know large sections of it off by heart. It is almost certain that they knew the Old Testament better than most Bible school graduates today.

We know this, not least, because the New Testament often assumes this level of knowledge of its readers. For example, Paul in 1 Corinthians 5 addresses the problem of a church member co-habiting with his step-mother. Deuteronomy 22 details various aspects of sexual immorality, some of which carried the death penalty. In that chapter, Moses said, 'you shall purge the evil person from Israel.' Verse 30 of that chapter says: 'A man shall not take his father's wife'—the precise situation Paul was addressing at Corinth. When Paul says in the last verse of chapter 5, 'Purge the evil person from among you,' he never mentions Deuteronomy, or even that he is citing the Old Testament. But what he writes, in Greek, is almost exactly word for word the same as the Deuteronomy 22 verse in the Greek translation of the Old Testament (known as the Septuagint or LXX). It seems clear that Paul expected the church at Corinth, even though it was a Gentile church far from Palestine, to know that verse, and to understand his logic: if Moses wanted such a person out of Israel, surely we do not want such a person in the church at Corinth, and so he should be expelled.

In summary, as modern-day interpreters of Scripture, if we are to get at the original author's meaning we need to be sensitive to the possibility of allusions to other texts, incidents, or concepts, that might not be immediately obvious to us, but might have been clear to the original readers.

1.6   A Wrong Turn

In Matthew 24:1–2 Jesus prophesies a cataclysmic destruction of Jerusalem:

> Jesus left the temple and was going away, when his disciples came to point out to him the buildings of the temple. But he answered them, "You see all these, do you not? Truly, I say to you, there will not be left here one stone upon another that will not be thrown down."

In 70 CE Caesar commanded his armies to destroy the entire city leaving no building standing—contemporary reports say that more than a million men, women, and children were murdered. So great was the destruction that much of Jewish culture, including how they understood their own Scriptures, was lost to subsequent generations.

Even before 70 CE, many Jewish people no longer knew Hebrew, most now speaking Aramaic (possibly including Jesus himself)—therefore the Hebrew Bible had been translated into Greek. This translation gave many Greek philosophers access to the Old Testament for the first time and some, notably Philo, took to writing commentaries on it. Philo believed, like Plato had in an earlier century, that there was an invisible world that formed the pattern for our world—ideas that became to be known as 'neoplatonic.' Philo used these neoplatonic ideas in his own writings about the story of Adam and Eve in Genesis, and saw that Adam is the prototype of man as a husband, Eve the prototype of woman as a wife.[8]

The Christian church was in its infancy and now living in a world that was dominated by Graeco-Roman culture. It had the Greek Old Testament that the contemporary Greek philosophers were giving their views on, and its own Greek New Testament. Richard Hays comments that, 'Christian tradition early on lost its vital connection with the Jewish interpretative matrix in which Paul had lived and moved.'[9] It was not long before the church began to absorb some of these neoplatonic ideas—and over the subsequent centuries the church's understanding of marriage and divorce became a mixture of Greek philosophy, Roman law, and biblical teaching.[10]

From this cultural mix came the idea that, as with Adam and Eve, each individual marriage is made by God, and thus marriage has a mystical dimension—in other words, when a couple marry on earth, it is a reflection of something that has happened in heaven. This understanding was adopted by the newly emerging Church of Rome. That Church, early in its development, came to believe that it alone can mediate things happening in heaven, and so it was logical, if marriage had a heavenly dimension, that marriage had to be considered a sacrament and thus administered by a priest.

These ideas developed over the centuries, and although it was not until 1563 that this teaching was formalised by the Church of Rome, this was the teaching and practice of the Church long before that date. It meant that nobody was considered married unless a priest performed the ceremony.

This concept of a heavenly, or at least a mystical, dimension to marriage lives on even in the secular world in the West today, where people sometimes speak of a 'marriage made in heaven.'

This has resulted in what Quentin Skinner says on a different but related matter, that there is often an:

> unconscious application of paradigms whose familiarity to the historian disguises an essential inapplicability to the past … it seems clear that at least a part of [any] understanding must lie in grasping what sort of society the given author was writing for and trying to persuade.[11]

Carol Meyers, when discussing the role of women in ancient Israel society, comments:

> The attitudes engendered by the Judeo-Christian tradition are so well entrenched in contemporary religion that they constitute powerful barriers to an understanding of the antecedent functions of certain texts in Israelite life.[12]

In other words, these scholars are saying that when we read the Bible text, our tendency is to read into it a modern Western understanding, an understanding that would have been quite alien to the original authors. Consequently, many Christians think that the neoplatonic idea, that the Adam and Eve marriage is the marriage model for all men and women, and that earthly marriage has a heavenly dimension, is the understanding of the New Testament writers themselves. But our ever-increasing knowledge of the ancient world, and particularly the Jewish marriage documents from New Testament times that have been discovered in the last 60 years, demonstrate that this is extremely unlikely.

Those documents make it clear that the traditions that have developed in Judeo-Christian culture over the years in the West concerning marriage, divorce, and remarriage do not relate to the understanding of marriage in New Testament times. And our modern mindset, so greatly influenced by Graeco-Roman philosophy and culture, has made it difficult for us to make sense of New Testament teaching on the subject.

Perhaps we should have been more alert to this, as the New Testament is laden with direct quotations from, and allusions to, not secular philosophy, but the Old Testament. Indeed, the New Testament makes no sense without the Old Testament. Furthermore, as mentioned above, Jesus lived and taught as a Jew, and Paul himself, whose writings form so much of the New Testament, could say as already mentioned, 'I stand here ... saying nothing but what the prophets and Moses said would come to pass' (Acts 26:22).

Despite the Reformation in the 16th and 17th centuries, and its *sola scriptura* (only Scripture) principle, the Reformers did not have access to the world that the apostles lived in. Although they challenged the idea that marriage was a sacrament, some key elements of the neoplatonic understanding of marriage that the early post-apostolic church had adopted, and its associated teaching about divorce and remarriage, survived largely intact.

The fact that there is now nearly 2,000 years of history behind this teaching has meant it is firmly planted in our minds—many Christians sincerely believing that this is what the New Testament itself teaches. This book is an attempt to help us see the New Testament divorce and remarriage teaching in its context, as evidenced in the Bible's marital imagery, and the contemporary social and literary context that that imagery relies on.

1.7   A Living Word

It might be thought that the need for such a contextually sensitive exegetical approach means that we must consider the Bible a 'dead' historical book with little relevance for today. However, Hebrews 4:12 says:

> For the word of God is living and active, sharper than any two-edged sword, piercing to the division of soul and of spirit, of joints and of marrow, and discerning the thoughts and intentions of the heart.

And this is certainly the experience of every true Christian. But to get at the significance of what is being said the context is often required. For example, in Matthew 22 the disciples asked Jesus if it was lawful to pay taxes to Caesar, and when shown a coin with Caesar's head on it, Jesus said 'render unto Caesar what is Caesar's.' Jesus's teaching has wide ranging implications for our attitude to the secular state in our contemporary world today. But neither the question, nor the answer, would have made sense unless we understood that the Romans were an occupying power in Israel, and that Caesar was the Roman emperor. And in the book of Hebrews, which in our verse as above, describes the word of God as 'living and active,' there are so many references and allusions to the Old Testament that the book makes little sense without its Old Testament context.

1.8   The Clarity of Scripture

It might be further thought with the exegetical approach outlined in this chapter, that the Bible is extremely difficult to understand for any modern reader, and contradicts the concept of the clarity of Scripture. But we need to be clear what is meant by that. The Westminster Confession of Faith (§1.7) states:

> All things in Scripture are not alike plain in themselves, nor alike clear unto all (2 Pet. 3:16); yet those things which are necessary to be known, believed, and observed for salvation, are so clearly propounded, and opened in some place of Scripture or other, that not only the learned, but the unlearned, in a due use of the ordinary means, may attain unto a sufficient understanding of them.

The Confession is saying that not everything is immediately clear in the Bible. Indeed, if it was, there would be no need for us to have teachers in the church. We all, even (especially) teachers, need to learn, and keep learning. Paul chides the Christians at Corinth that they were acting as if they had understood 'all mysteries' (1 Corinthians 13:2), and says of them:

> But I, brothers, could not address you as spiritual people, but as people of the flesh, as infants in Christ. I fed you with milk, not solid food, for you were not ready for it. And even now you are not yet ready. (1 Corinthians 3:1–2)

And the letter to the Hebrews has:

> For though by this time you ought to be teachers, you need someone to teach you again the basic principles of the oracles of God. You need milk, not solid food, for everyone who lives on milk is unskilled in the word of righteousness, since he is a child. (Hebrews 5:12–13)

Considering the wide-ranging pastoral consequences of remaining as 'baby' Christians, it is surely incumbent on us all, and especially church leaders and teachers, to study the Bible in light of the principles that have been outlined above, and be like the Bereans, who:

> were more noble than those in Thessalonica; they received the word
> with all eagerness, examining the Scriptures daily to see if these
> things were so. (Acts 17:11)

1.9   Summary

Any evangelical surely believes that the New Testament writers' thought they were being clear, and that we have their teaching accurately represented in the text of Scripture that has come down to us today. The widely divergent range of traditional views on the Bible's divorce and remarriage teaching is clear testimony that the New Testament on this matter has been misunderstood. The root cause of this misunderstanding is that the church historically has failed to come to terms with the exegetical principles outlined in this chapter. However, if these principles are applied to the New Testament divorce and remarriage teaching, it will be seen that, in all its essential aspects, the New Testament is perfectly clear. Clear—but a challenge to many of the traditional views held today.

Some key points

1. The Bible is the living word of God and speaks to us today.

2. In all points pertaining to our salvation it is clear.

3. Nonetheless, to properly understand what God is saying, the context of the actual words used in the sentence, the context of the sentence in the passage, and the passage in the wider context of the Bible story, and the cultural context of that story, will all need to be considered.

Some questions

1. Is this the way you, your church, or the wider Christian community views the Bible?

2. What do you think the role of the church versus Bible schools/seminaries is in providing well equipped teachers and leaders who are able, as 2 Timothy 2:15 says, to 'rightly handle the word of truth'?

Chapter 2: Genesis 2:24

2.1 Introduction

> Therefore a man shall leave his father and his mother and hold fast
> to his wife, and they shall become one flesh. (Genesis 2:24)

In Genesis 2:24 God outlines the pattern for marriage for all humanity. If we
misunderstand this verse, it is rather like setting out on a journey with
sincere intentions, but with the wrong map. This is what I suggest happened
in the post-apostolic church—they merged, or we might say conflated, Adam
and Eve's marriage in Genesis 2:23, with the pattern for marriage in Genesis
2:24. The outcome was that the church understood Adam and Eve's marriage
as the model for humanity, and that understanding has gone largely
unchallenged since. But if the principles of chapter 1 are employed, and the
Bible text looked at carefully, it can be seen that the two marriages, and the
principles underlying them, are in fact quite different. We will look at the
two marriages in their original context now.

2.2 Two Marriages in Eden

> The man gave names to all livestock and to the birds of the heavens
> and to every beast of the field. But for Adam there was not found a
> helper fit for him. So the LORD God caused a deep sleep to fall upon
> the man, and while he slept took one of his ribs and closed up its
> place with flesh. And the rib that the LORD God had taken from the
> man he made into a woman and brought her to the man. Then the
> man said, "This at last is bone of my bones and flesh of my flesh; she
> shall be called Woman, because she was taken out of Man."
> Therefore a man shall leave his father and his mother and hold fast
> to his wife, and they shall become one flesh. (Genesis 2:20–24)

It is possible to immediately identify several clear differences between Adam
and Eve's marriage and how ordinary marriages are formed. Not least, for
that first couple, there was no courtship, and at their wedding (if it can be
called such), there were no witnesses, and seemingly no vows. But there are
other subtler and more profound differences, as we shall see.

2.3   To Become 'One Flesh'

Both Adam and Eve were miraculously created by God. Their formation and union were part of the sequence of events when God created the world, after which he 'rested' (Genesis 2:2). In contrast, Genesis 2:24 seems to be a reference to the ordinary cycle of life, speaking of a naturally born couple, and a man leaving his father and mother to join his wife. In this marriage, the couple *become* 'one flesh'—in other words, something has changed. This contrasts with Adam and Eve who always were the same flesh. This fact seems to be confirmed by the Hebrew, the original language of the Old Testament, in that it says in Genesis 2:23 that Eve came *from* Adam, but in Genesis 2:24 it says that the married couple come *into* their relationship. Furthermore, the Genesis 2:24 union is formed by the couple themselves, they choose each other. By way of contrast, for Adam and Eve, there was no choice—Eve, in the words of the old song, really was 'the only girl in the world' for Adam. This contrast between the two marriages has been somewhat clouded in our English translations when 'therefore' is used to introduce the Genesis 2:24 marriage, rather than the equally valid 'after that' —that is, after Adam and Eve's marriage something different is to happen.

But what is meant by the phrase: 'they shall become one flesh'? Flesh (*basar*) in biblical Hebrew often means 'family.' In the West today, we have a similar concept when we might say of a relation, 'they are my own flesh and blood.' In the Bible, it can also mean a broader grouping of a clan or kindred group— this can be seen in Leviticus 25:49 where ESV translates *basar* as 'clan.' Bruce Kaye states:

> The term "flesh and bone" occurs only eight times in the Old Testament apart from Genesis 2:23. In Genesis 29:14 and 37:27 it directly and clearly means someone who is a close blood relation.... In general terms, the phrase has the immediate and direct sense of blood relation but, as well, is used figuratively of a close relationship.[13]

David Instone-Brewer is a leading expert on the understanding of biblical Hebrew and was on the translation committee of the 2011 revision of the New International Version of the Bible—he comments that in ancient Israel:

'"they shall be one flesh" would probably have been interpreted to mean "they shall be one family."'[14]

Thus it is clear from the Old Testament that the one-flesh union of Genesis 2:24 was in ancient Israel considered to be a *one family* union: husband and wife were, on marriage, perceived to be 'kin.' Even though they shared no blood, the new family is seen to be a cohesive unit—such being formed by a voluntary agreement (what we might term a *volitional covenant*) between the husband and wife. In contrast, Adam and Eve were already (literally!) 'one flesh' before they came together in a marriage—nothing changed for them, and there appears to have been no vows—in other words, there was no covenant.

What is more, Adam and Eve must have shared the same blood—their relationship was what is known as a *consanguineous* relationship (in contrast to a marital *affinity* union). Such a marriage to a blood relation is forbidden in the Bible, and thus we find another aspect of their relationship that cannot be the blueprint for subsequent marriages.

These two different relationships (consanguine and affinity) are found in any family with birth children, and can be mapped like this:

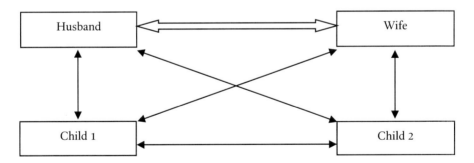

The parent/child/brother/sister relationships in any family with birth (as opposed to adopted) children are blood relationships (i.e. consanguineous) and in that sense, they are like Adam and Eve, in that these relationships are (and always were) one flesh. They are not created by choice, they are not based on a covenant, and are permanent—a reality, not a construct. In contrast, the Genesis 2:24 one-flesh relationship between the husband and wife is a construct of a covenantal union. This newly created union, despite not being consanguineous, is *counted as* being consanguineous in the Bible, in that certain sexual relationships are now forbidden to the new family, as outlined in Leviticus chapters 18 and 20. We might say that the Genesis 2:24 one-flesh union is a *metaphoric* one-flesh union—in other words not literally, but counted as, being 'one flesh.' In fact, Genesis 2:24 has the classic metaphoric A 'is' B non-literal statement—the couple 'is' (are rather become) a one flesh union. The vehicle of this metaphor is a consanguineous union, the tenor is the affinity union of the married couple.

2.4   A Summary

We have seen that a contextually sensitive understanding of Genesis 2:24 is:

> After that [i.e. in contrast to Adam and Eve], a man shall leave his father and his mother and hold fast to his wife, and they shall become [by means of a covenant] one family.

We can now set out some of the key differences between Adam and Eve's marriage, with its literal one-flesh relationship, and the metaphoric one-flesh union formed by a couple when they choose to be married:

Genesis 2:23	Genesis 2:24
1. A miraculous man and woman.	1. A naturally born man and woman.
2. Remain as they are.	2. Choose to become what they were not.
3. In a literal one-flesh union.	3. In a metaphoric one-flesh union.
4. Without the need for a covenant.	4. By means of a covenant.

Despite these clear differences, the Christian church has conflated these two marriages, so that when Genesis 2:24 is referred to in either the Old Testament or the New Testament, many believe that the verse refers to Adam and Eve. This has meant that many Bible exegetes see the model for our marriages is Adam and Eve's union. For example, a leading Old Testament scholar says that Genesis 2:24, 'is a comment by the narrator applying the principles of the first marriage to every marriage';[15] however, the four principles of Genesis 2:24 outlined above are mutually exclusive to the principles underlying Genesis 2:23 and the first marriage described there.

In the next chapter, our task is to look at marriage and divorce in the Old Testament to see if it fits with the pattern of marriage God has laid out in Genesis 2:24.

———————————————

Some key points

1. Adam and Eve's marriage was miraculously formed by God. Their creation and marriage formed part of the creation week. It was a unique event in the history of our world which has never been repeated.

2. Thus Adam and Eve's marriage is not the model for our marriages.

3. Instead, when a couple who do not have a close blood relationship, choose to marry, they form an affinity relationship by committing to each other by means of their wedding vows. In other words, their marriage is a metaphoric one-flesh (one family) union formed by a volitional covenant.

Some questions

1. Do you believe that having a 'model' or paradigm in our minds influences the way we understand a verse or passage of Scripture?

2. If it is accepted, at least at this early stage of this book, that Genesis 2:23 and Genesis 2:24 have been conflated by scholars and the church, how do you think it is possible for such a misunderstanding of the Bible's teaching to occur, when we believe his word is clear?

3. Can you think of other examples where many Christians now believe that the church, in the past, has misunderstood the Bible?

4. How do we reconcile any such misunderstandings with God's providence?

Chapter 3: Marriage and Divorce in the Old Testament

3.1 Introduction

In Genesis 2:23 we are told that Adam and Eve were brought together by God and their union formed by him. We now turn to the Old Testament to see how a new marital 'one flesh/one family' affinity union came about in ancient Israel, and in the process, we can learn about the Old Testament understanding of divorce and remarriage.

3.2 Marriage Law

Ancient Israel was a theocracy and a great many aspects of daily life were regulated by the more than 600 Pentateuchal laws, and dominated by the cycle of tabernacle/temple ceremonies controlled by the priesthood.

The Pentateuchal legislation is sometimes set out in the form of general principles (for example, the Ten Commandments), but it is more often articulated in the form of a 'protasis' and 'apodosis.' In other words, if such and such happened, then this is the rule. So, for example, Deuteronomy says what is to be done if a woman is taken in battle as a wife (Deuteronomy 21); or there is sexual immorality (Deuteronomy 22); if a husband divorces his wife, she marries another, and her second marriage also ends (Deuteronomy 24); or a brother dies without children (Deuteronomy 25).

These hypothetical examples were used as the basis of laws. It is rather like in the UK when a judgement in a court trial sets a precedent and becomes part of UK case law. These Pentateuchal hypothetical examples were, in effect, treated like judgements in a trial, and case laws were made based on them—often using what is known as the *qal va-chomer* (from light to heavy) principle. An example of Jesus making such a judgement is found in Matthew:

> And a man was there with a withered hand. And they asked him, "Is it lawful to heal on the Sabbath?"—so that they might accuse him. He said to them, "Which one of you who has a sheep, if it falls into a pit on the Sabbath, will not take hold of it and lift it out? Of how

much more value is a man than a sheep! So it is lawful to do good on the Sabbath." (Matthew 12:10–12)

Jesus's *qal va-chomer* argument is what applies to the sheep, must apply to a man, and thus healing on the Sabbath is lawful.

Exodus 21:7–11 is another example of a judgement based on a hypothetical situation, framed as a protasis and apodosis argument:

> When a man sells his daughter as a slave, she shall not go out as the male slaves do. If she does not please her master, who has designated her for himself, then he shall let her be redeemed. He shall have no right to sell her to a foreign people, since he has broken faith with her. If he designates her for his son, he shall deal with her as with a daughter. If he takes another wife to himself, he shall not diminish her food, her clothing, or her marital rights. And if he does not do these three things for her, she shall go out for nothing, without payment of money.

Thus a man sells his daughter into slavery in the expectation that either the master, or the master's son, will marry her. If neither of them marry her, she is not to be sold to foreigners. If the master marries her, but then marries another woman, the first (slave) wife is not to be denied food, clothes, or 'marital rights.'

Marital rights certainly referred to the conjugal rights of marriage, not least because having children, particularly in ancient times, was an integral expectation of marriage. But it seems it also meant that a wife was entitled to a wider emotional support—in other words, as today, the sexual act alone was not considered to be the entire dimension of the marital relationship.

Although in Western culture men do not have slaves, or more than one wife, this teaching in Exodus 21, just a few verses from the Ten Commandments, formed the basis of the case law on marriage in ancient Israel. The *qal va-chomer* argument was if a slave wife was entitled to those things, how much more so a free wife. What is more, there is a strong indication from the passage itself that this deduction is valid—verse 9 says:

'if he designates her for his son, he shall deal with her as with a daughter'—implying that a daughter, as a free woman, would expect to be treated no less well than a slave woman.

And thus the marriage law in ancient Israel was that a husband had binding duties to provide for his wife. This commitment is found written into every surviving marriage contract from New Testament times, and it will be seen below that any failure by a husband to provide for his wife as outlined in the 'triad' of care in Exodus 21, was considered sufficient grounds for a wife to divorce him.

Nonetheless, it seems that marriage was a private matter between the couple themselves and their respective families, and was not mediated by any priest or elder—there appears to have been no religious or state involvement of any kind. So while it was understood that marriage formed part of God's purpose for humanity, the absence of any religious ceremony indicates that there was not a concept that God formed *each* marriage. Despite the lack of clarity about the nature of any specific wedding vows and ceremonies, the nature of the marriage agreement in ancient Israel emerges from its narrative accounts.

3.3   Marriage in the Narratives

In the Old Testament record, after Eden, the first marriage referenced is in Genesis 4:17 where Cain's wife is mentioned without further elaboration as to her origin, or any associated marital procedure. It is not until Genesis 24 that some account is found of a process or custom attached to the marriage union, where Abraham seeks a wife for his son Isaac, 'from my kindred' (Genesis 24:4). This marriage (or at least the selection of the bride) involved divine intervention. But Abraham was a prophet, and supernatural guidance was given via an angel to achieve God's specific purposes for the nation Israel—there is no indication that this was to be the norm.[16]

Family involvement in the choice of partner seems to be a mark of marriages in many ancient cultures, and arranged marriages were probably common. Despite the widely-held view in the West that the principal reason for marriage is love, this is not the Old Testament perspective. The references to love in marriage appear only infrequently. However, Isaac is said to have loved Rebekah (Genesis 24:67); Jacob loved Rachel (Genesis 29:18); and

Michal loved David (1 Samuel 18:20). Samson's love for Delilah is recorded in Judges 16:4, but it is not clear that they ever married.

But there are no examples in the Bible of a marriage against the will of the bride (except in the cases of a slave wife, Exodus 21:7–11, or a woman taken in a battle, Deuteronomy 21:10–14), or against the will of the groom. Marriages in ancient Israel were formed when a couple chose to be married, and scholars point out that a covenant, that is, an agreement (usually given verbally, or simply implied), was the essence of such a marriage.

However, the word 'covenant' has come to have special significance in Christian tradition, and the employment of that word in Malachi 2:14 is often appealed to as evidence that marriage in the Old Testament was indeed formed by a 'covenant,' understood in its Christian sense of a solemn, unbreakable commitment, made before God:

> Because the LORD was witness between you and the wife of your youth, to whom you have been faithless, though she is your companion and your wife by covenant. (Malachi 2:14)

But not only is the Hebrew text very unclear, it will be suggested in §4.7 that Malachi is referring to God's own relationship with Israel, not to human marriage.

In fact, there is not a single clear instance in the Bible of human marriage being declared to be a covenant. And what is more, the word 'covenant' (in Hebrew, *berit*) had no special significance in ancient Israel, it simply meant contract. In other words, what made any contract/covenant significant were the terms of the covenant and the parties involved, not the use of the word *berit*, and Instone-Brewer argues persuasively that marriage 'contract' better conveys the Old Testament meaning of the marriage agreement.[17] Notwithstanding that, this book will use the word covenant, but only in the context of its meaning an agreement, or contract.

3.4   Betrothal and Bride-price

A marriage was preceded by a betrothal, when the bridegroom would pay to the bride's father a sum of money, called in Hebrew the *mohar*, an example is in Exodus 22:17 (where ESV translates *mohar* as 'bride-price'). In some cases, it seems that the money would then be passed to the bride by her father for the couple to use in their life together. That money would nonetheless be considered to belong to the wife and she could take it with her if she was widowed or divorced. The West is more familiar with a dowry, where the bride's father gives her a sum of money on marriage. However, the giving of a *mohar* is still evidenced in many cultures today—from my personal experience this includes West Africa and Madagascar.

The payment of the *mohar* starts the betrothal period, and eventually (it might be a year or more) the bridegroom would come for his bride, and the marriage consummated. While the sexual consummation of the marriage was obviously a key aspect, there is no evidence to suggest that such was considered to be the essence of marriage, as it is perceived to be in some Christian traditions today. We will return to this point in §6.6.

It was normal in Israel for the bride to re-locate to her husband's family home where she would then belong. This process is symbolised in the West today when the bride often takes her husband's family name. Thus the comment in Genesis 2:24 that a man was to 'leave his father and mother' is unlikely to mean that he leaves his family home—it is probably a reference to the fact that the new husband is to 'forsake' his family, that is, to start a new family that has a new set of responsibilities and emotional ties for him.

It will be seen in §5.5 that the *mohar* tradition, and its associated betrothal period, is a fundamental aspect of New Testament marital imagery. In that imagery, Jesus comes to our home to pay the *mohar* on the cross and secure his bride, the church, and one day he will return to take her to his own home.

It will be remembered that in all the Bible's marital imagery we are being asked to *imagine* God is married and/or betrothed to his people. In that imagery, God's marriage is based on the Bible's teaching, and on marital practices from actual marriages in biblical times. It follows that this is how God himself understood marriage should be. His marriage included betrothal—he sent his Son, the Lord Jesus Christ, to betroth the church. It might be noted that in Adam and Eve's marriage there is no *mohar* payment, or a betrothal period—another indication that their marriage was not considered to be a model for our own.

However, betrothal is but one example of a human marital tradition found in the biblical imagery but *not* in Adam and Eve's marriage. In fact, it will be seen that nothing is utilised from the primal couple marriage as a pattern for God's marriage (excepting at the very closing verses of Revelation, see §5.7). God's marriage to his people is a Genesis 2:24 marriage.

3.5   Divorce

Divorce for the Husband

The grounds for divorce in the Old Testament were gender specific. The husband's grounds for divorce are found in Deuteronomy:

> When a man takes a wife and marries her, if then she finds no favour in his eyes because he has found some indecency in her, and he writes her a certificate of divorce and puts it in her hand and sends her out of his house, and she departs out of his house, and if she goes and becomes another man's wife, and the latter man hates her and writes her a certificate of divorce and puts it in her hand and sends her out of his house, or if the latter man dies, who took her to be his wife, then her former husband, who sent her away, may not take her again to be his wife, after she has been defiled, for that is an abomination before the LORD. And you shall not bring sin upon the land that the LORD your God is giving you for an inheritance. (Deuteronomy 24:1–4)

This protasis/apodosis argument states that a man can divorce his wife for any 'indecency,' and that she is free to remarry once he has given her the required certificate. But if she does marry again, and that marriage ends in a divorce (for whatever reason), she cannot come back to her first husband. From this passage, it was understood that a man was free to divorce his wife if she was guilty of any indecency. What 'indecency' meant became the subject of debate among the Pharisees in New Testament times and so we will consider this in more detail in §7.2.

The fact that the husband had to give the certificate has led many to deduce that in the Old Testament only the husband could initiate a divorce, but this is to confuse the right to initiate a divorce with the right to issue the certificate. Either partner had the right to initiate a divorce, but only the husband could issue the certificate—it is the equivalent of the UK *decree absolute* which enables either partner to remarry. In Israel divorce was still a divorce without any certificate. But adultery was a capital offence, and any prospective husband of a divorced woman would be very keen to know that the previous marriage had truly ended, and so would need to see the certificate. The whole purpose of this certificate was to free the wife to enable her to remarry. In the UK, it is the judge that issues the certificate, but in ancient Israel marriage (and divorce) was a private arrangement between husband and wife and their respective families.

Divorce for the Wife

The freedom for a wife to leave a marriage is not reflected in the teaching of most of the traditional views of divorce today. But virtually all the marriage contracts that have been found throughout the Ancient Near East, dating from 2000 BCE, right through to New Testament times, have a clause that state, or imply, that the husband was to provide the Exodus 'triad' of obligations as above. And specifically, the marriage contracts dating from New Testament times that were discovered between 1951 and 1962 to the west of the Dead Sea (The Judaean Desert Documents), are considered by all scholars who have examined them to accurately reflect Jewish life in New Testament times, and all articulate the Exodus triad of obligation as the essence of a husband's duties.

In contrast, the wife's duties are not articulated in the text of the Old Testament, or in any surviving marriage documents. It seems that such were so taken for granted that they were not recorded. But they can be readily deduced, as the sole basis for a husband initiating a divorce was his wife's sexual impurity, as explained in Deuteronomy 24:1–4. The essence of a wife's duty was to provide her husband with his (and not another's man's) children.

It might be thought that this was an unfair dual standard in that a husband's requirement for sexual faithfulness is not articulated in the Old Testament marital legislation—it would not be considered immoral in ancient Israel, as in many Ancient Near East cultures, if a man took a never-married, divorced, or widowed woman as a second wife. Although strange to us, it must be remembered that there was no social provision from the state in the Ancient Near East, and male life expectancy was often very short. A single woman's life could be very difficult, and the acceptance of polygyny (i.e., having more than one wife) in these societies was often a means of ensuring that every woman who wanted a husband and children, or support as a widow, had a greatly increased opportunity of achieving that. In these ancient societies, it was rare to be an unmarried woman by choice.

And it might be noted that the Exodus 21 passage gave the slave wife the right to leave the marriage if her husband took another wife. In effect, he could only take another wife with the first wife's permission, and in some surviving marriage contracts the wife stipulates from the outset of the marriage that the husband was not to take another wife.

3.6   Summary

The Old Testament record demonstrates that in ancient Israel marriage and divorce was a private matter without any involvement of the priesthood, tabernacle or temple—it was not considered to have a religious dimension. Rather, it was a conditional, volitional, asymmetrical contract based on the principles of Genesis 2:24—a couple were considered on marriage to be 'one flesh'—that is, a new family unit. Divorce could be initiated by either partner, but only the husband could issue the certificate to enable a divorced wife to remarry.

Some key points

1. The volitional, conditional, covenantal marriage described in Genesis 2:24 is the basis for all Old Testament marriages after that first marriage of Adam and Eve.

2. Marriage was not considered a 'sacrament'—in other words, it was not seen to have a heavenly dimension, or to be a union formed with God as a witness, and thus no priest or religious ceremony was involved in forming a marriage.

3. Divorce could be initiated by either partner, but only the husband could issue the certificate to enable a divorced wife to remarry.

Some questions

1. Why do you think that the teaching of Exodus 21 has been largely ignored by the Christian church?

2. Do you think that in our modern society the church family at least complements the role of a believer's natural family, and this might justify a church ceremony, even though there is no example of such in the Bible?

Chapter 4: God the Husband of Israel

4.1   Introduction

In §1.4 we considered large scale metaphors, and gave as an example: THE LORD IS MY SHEPHERD. But there is one metaphor that dominates the Old Testament story, and it is GOD IS THE HUSBAND OF ISRAEL. In fact, there is more devoted to this *Divine Marriage* in the Old Testament than any teaching about, or description of, human marriages. The Old Testament scholar Raymond Westbrook comments:

> If God's relationship with Israel is to be explained by a metaphor drawing upon the everyday life of the audience then that metaphor, to be effective, must reflect accurately the reality known to the audience. If the narrator were to invent the legal rules on which the metaphor is based, it would cease to be a valid metaphor.[18]

He is saying that for the imagery to make sense, for people to understand what God is saying about his relationship to Israel, the imagery must be based on Israel's understanding of marriage. In metaphoric terms, human marriage as understood in Israel, is the source domain that populates the target domain—the *Divine Marriage*.

Although in the previous chapter we have already looked at Old Testament marriage teaching, it is hoped by spending a short time looking at how God's own marriage is portrayed in the Old Testament, we can understand more about how God thinks a human marriage should work.[19] We will then try to draw lessons from these Old Testament concepts of marriage and divorce in our approach to the New Testament marriage teaching, where our focus will be on divorce and remarriage.

GOD IS THE HUSBAND OF ISRAEL, is the root metaphor of the Old Testament marital imagery, and from that root metaphor many consequent analogies flow. They can be mapped like this:

MAP 3 GOD IS THE HUSBAND OF ISRAEL

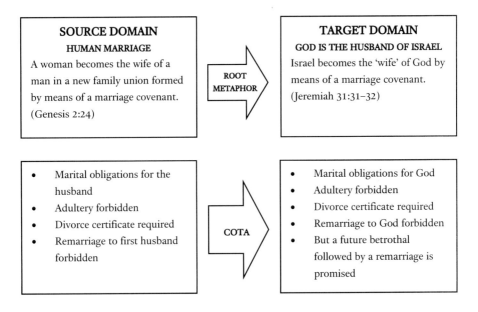

COTA = Consequent Old Testament Analogies

4.2 A Marriage at Sinai

Although many believe that it is Hosea who introduced and developed the idea that God is 'married' to his people, others see that the concept of a *Divine Marriage* goes further back in the Old Testament. For example, Instone-Brewer suggests that Hosea's marital imagery was not developed in a vacuum and that the 'whole language of "jealousy," which is central to the picture of God in the Pentateuch, has the connotation of marriage' and that Sinai can be seen as the point at which God marries his people.[20]

Exodus 34:15–16, Leviticus 17:7; 20:5–6, Numbers 25:1, and Deuteronomy 31:16, speak about Israel 'whoring' after other gods—in other words they were not being faithful to their 'husband'—and in Deuteronomy 33:3 Moses says that God 'loved his people.' All these verses suggest marital imagery. Furthermore, in ancient Semitic societies marriage is often signified when the verb to take (*lqḥ*) is used, so it is perhaps not without significance that the same verb is used in Exodus 6:7 ('I will take you to be my people') to express God's choice of Israel. And at Sinai, the account of the golden calf being ground to powder and the people being forced to drink it (Exodus 32:20) is possibly a reference to the Numbers 5:12–31 ordeal for the suspected adulteress. It seems that Israel had been unfaithful on her 'wedding night.' In addition, both Hosea 2:14–15 and Jeremiah 2:2–3 look back to the desert wanderings after Sinai as the 'honeymoon' period in Yahweh's relationship with Israel—and God specifically refers to himself as the husband of Israel in Jeremiah 31:31–32:

> Behold, the days are coming, declares the Lord, when I will make a
> new covenant with the house of Israel and the house of Judah, not
> like the covenant that I made with their fathers on the day when I
> took them by the hand to bring them out of the land of Egypt, my
> covenant that they broke, though I was their husband, declares
> the Lord. (Jeremiah 31:31–32)

4.3   God's Covenant with Israel

There are several covenants or covenant-like relationships between God and his people in the Old Testament which carry theological significance, among them the Edenic (Genesis 1:26–30; 2:15–17), Adamic (Genesis 3:14–19), Noahic (Genesis 9:1–17), Abrahamic (Genesis 12:1–3, 7; 13:14–17; 15:1–21; 17:1–21), Sinaitic (Exodus 19–24), and Davidic (2 Samuel 7:5–16)—so a key to understanding the relationship between God and Israel (described in the OT as a marriage), is to understand the basis of that Sinaitic covenant. Dennis McCarthy points out that the promissory, unconditional covenants (examples might include those with Abraham and David), and the conditional covenants, are different from each other, and states, 'the attempt to make the Davidic covenant formally identical with the Mosaic on the basis of a covenant form common to the two has failed.'[21]

The Sinaitic covenant, was *volitional*, that is, Israel had choices, both at the outset (e.g. Exodus 19:3–8; Exodus 24:3–8; Deuteronomy 30:11–20), and later (e.g. Joshua 24:1–28)—Joshua's speech seemingly containing real options for Israel many years after Sinai. McCarthy comments that, 'the people are asked, never compelled, to enter into the relationship.'[22] The Sinaitic covenant, was also *conditional*. 'If' is a much-repeated word in this covenant—this conditionality is encapsulated in Exodus 19:5, 'Now therefore, if you will indeed obey my voice and keep my covenant, you shall be my treasured possession among all peoples, for all the earth is mine.' Thus the Sinaitic covenant is volitional *and* conditional—a contractual agreement based on Israel's obedience and her own desire to remain in the covenant. And it is this covenant that is portrayed as a marriage in the Old Testament. McCarthy states that, 'the husband-wife relationship between Yahweh and Israel … is, of course, a contractual relationship.'[23]

The relationship between God and Israel expressed in the Sinaitic covenant is consistent with the concept of a volitional, conditional, covenantal human marriage—and both are consistent with the marriage described in Genesis 2:24. What is more, Israel as a nation *became* the people of God at Sinai—in other words they *became what they were not*, a key feature of a Genesis 2:24 marriage. Indeed, none of the features of Adam and Eve's marriage are found in the Sinaitic covenant or the *Divine Marriage*. God's 'marriage' with Israel as portrayed throughout the Old Testament is a Genesis 2:24 marriage.

4.4 A Marriage in Eden

It is possible that the Bible's marital imagery goes even further back than the covenant at Sinai. Several scholars have seen parallels between the Garden of Eden and the events recorded there, and the story of Israel in the Promised Land—the covenantal nature of God's relationship with Adam seems to be a pre-echo of God's 'marriage' with Israel at Sinai. For example:

Adam is placed in a garden that will supply all his needs.	Israel is placed in the promised land, a land 'flowing with milk and honey.'
However, in the garden there was a serpent that caused Adam to sin.	However, in the land were Canaanites who caused the Israelites to sin.
Adam was ejected from the garden. Genesis 3:23–24 uses two Hebrew words that mean divorce.	Israel was ejected from the land. Jeremiah 3:1–8 specifically describes it as a divorce.
Adam is not allowed to return (Genesis 3:24).	Israel is not allowed to return (Jeremiah 3:1–8).

Thus Adam's exile from Eden is portrayed as a 'divorce' from God just as Israel's exile from the promised land is described as a divorce in Jeremiah 3:1–8. It is possible that Hosea 6:7 ('But like Adam they transgressed the covenant') is a reference to the same.

The exile from Eden implied that in some way Adam and Eve had become contaminated and so had to be dealt with in a manner that reflected the Leviticus 16 scapegoat ritual—once the goat had the sins of the nation laid upon it, it had to be excluded from the presence of God. There was to be a boundary between what is holy and what is not. Thus in a similar way, Adam, and all his progeny, had to be kept away from God by the 'flaming sword' of Genesis 3:24. This is another echo of the concept that God had been 'married' to Adam, as this permanent exclusion from Eden precisely reflects the Old Testament divorce teaching of Deuteronomy 24, where a woman once divorced could not go back to her first husband—verse 4 says it would be an 'abomination before the LORD' (Deuteronomy 24 is discussed in §3.5; §7.2; §7.4).

4.5   God's Divorce in Hosea

However, the marital imagery first appears prominently in the book of Hosea, which tells the story of the prophet Hosea being told to marry a promiscuous woman, Gomer. At times the imagery is quite complex, as Gomer, the land, and the children of the marriage, all appear as symbols for the people of Israel and Judah. But the overall message is clear: God is saying to Hosea that the difficult relationship you will have with your wife, is like my relationship with the people of Israel and Judah. Chapter 1 describes it like this:

> When the LORD first spoke through Hosea, the LORD said to Hosea, "Go, take to yourself a wife of whoredom and have children of whoredom, for the land commits great whoredom by forsaking the LORD." So he went and took Gomer, the daughter of Diblaim, and she conceived and bore him a son. And the LORD said to him, "Call his name Jezreel, for in just a little while I will punish the house of Jehu for the blood of Jezreel, and I will put an end to the kingdom of the house of Israel. And on that day I will break the bow of Israel in the Valley of Jezreel." She conceived again and bore a daughter. And the LORD said to him, "Call her name No Mercy, for I will no more have mercy on the house of Israel, to forgive them at all. But I will have mercy on the house of Judah, and I will save them by the LORD their God. I will not save them by bow or by sword or by war or by

horses or by horsemen." When she had weaned No Mercy, she conceived and bore a son. [And the LORD said, "Call his name Not My People, for you are not my people, and I am not your God." (Hosea 1:2–9)

Hosea is saying that Israel is going to be separated from God—they will be called 'Not My People' (v. 9). In 722 BCE Israel was invaded and the ten northern tribes (usually called 'Israel' in the Old Testament) were taken to Assyria—it is this exile that is portrayed in the Old Testament marital imagery as a divorce. In v. 7 ('But I will have mercy on the house of Judah') Hosea tells us that Judah, unlike Israel (the ten northern tribes), will be spared. And then vv. 10–11 give a promise that looks forward to what was going to be accomplished in a new 'marriage':

> Yet the number of the children of Israel shall be like the sand of the sea, which cannot be measured or numbered. And in the place where it was said to them, "You are not my people," it shall be said to them, "Children of the living God." And the children of Judah and the children of Israel shall be gathered together, and they shall appoint for themselves one head. And they shall go up from the land, for great shall be the day of Jezreel. (Hosea 1:10–11)

We will see in chapter 5 that the New Testament marital imagery makes it clear that it is this marriage promise that the Lord Jesus Christ came to fulfil.

Some commentators find it difficult to believe that Hosea divorces Gomer, or that in the *Divine Marriage* God divorces Israel. But the declaration in Hosea 2:2, 'she is not my wife, and I am not her husband,' is known to be a divorce declaration used in the ancient world. What is more, the 'not my people' of Hosea 1:9 seems to be clearly saying that Israel are no longer to be considered God's people.

This perspective is in harmony with the divorce declaration of Hosea 2:2, and with 2:7, which says, 'Then she shall say, "I will go and return to my first husband, for it was better for me then than now."' And in vv. 8–9 Israel accepts that she would no longer receive the grain, wine, and oil which she had been entitled to as God's 'wife.'

Furthermore, despite William Dumbrell's view (consonant with other Old Testament exegetes from within the Christian community) that the covenant with Israel, 'could not be sundered'—he nonetheless sees that the Sinai covenant was tied to political forms and a territorial state, and that the stability of this depended upon Israel's response.[24]

Finally, it is difficult to see how Jeremiah could have been clearer when he says that Israel 'broke' the covenant:

> Behold, the days are coming, declares the Lord, when I will make a new covenant with the house of Israel and the house of Judah, not like the covenant that I made with their fathers on the day when I took them by the hand to bring them out of the land of Egypt, my covenant that they broke, though I was their husband, declares the Lord. (Jeremiah 31:31–32)

4.6   God's Divorce in Isaiah and Jeremiah

Both Isaiah and Jeremiah portray God as divorcing Israel, and specifically with reference to the Deuteronomy 24 human divorce legislation (cited in §3.5), that states that once the husband has given his wife the divorce certificate to release her to remarry, she could never come back to him.

In Isaiah chapter 50, the prophet speaks of Judah's exile to Babylon (c. 598 BCE), and in v. 1 God reassures them that, despite their exile, they had not suffered the same fate as divorced Israel:

> Thus says the LORD: "Where is your mother's certificate of divorce, with which I sent her away? Or which of my creditors is it to whom I have sold you? Behold, for your iniquities you were sold, and for your transgressions your mother was sent away."

God, through Isaiah, is challenging Judah to produce their divorce certificate. But it was a rhetorical question, because God knew they could not produce any such certificate. Furthermore, their 'mother,' (that is, the previous generation in Judah), had *not* been sold to any creditors, although they had indeed been sent away because of the nation's transgressions. Of course, this is marital *imagery*, something to be *imagined*, so there would never have been any literal certificate. But the point is clear—despite being exiled to Babylon, they had *not* been divorced. Thus Judah's exile is portrayed as a separation, in contrast to Israel's exile which is said to be a divorce. In Isaiah 51:2 we read, 'the LORD comforts Zion'—Judah is promised a reconciliation.

Jeremiah also addresses the issue of Israel's divorce, in 31:31–32 as above, and in chapter 3 he cites Deuteronomy 24 to explain that because of the broken covenant, what had happened to Israel *was* a divorce—she cannot come back to God. Jeremiah comments that Judah should have understood this, and learnt a lesson from it for herself, but she had not done so:

> If a man divorces his wife and she goes from him and becomes another man's wife, will he return to her? Would not that land be greatly polluted? You have played the whore with many lovers; and would you return to me? declares the LORD…. The LORD said to me in the days of King Josiah: "Have you seen what she did, that faithless one, Israel, how she went up on every high hill and under every green tree, and there played the whore? And I thought, 'After she has done all this she will return to me', but she did not return, and her treacherous sister Judah saw it. She saw that for all the adulteries of that faithless one, Israel, I had sent her away with a decree of divorce. Yet her treacherous sister Judah did not fear, but she too went and played the whore. (Jeremiah 3:1, 6–8)

We might paraphrase what Jeremiah is saying as, 'be careful Judah, unlike Israel (the ten northern tribes), you have not received the certificate (the certificate that any husband divorcing his wife had to give)—but if you do not improve I will surely divorce you also.'

Some might argue that even if God did divorce Israel, it does not mean that human divorce is valid. But that is to deny the very essence of the metaphor. We have seen that every metaphor has two halves, which we have called a source and target domain—one is based on the other, one illustrates the other. In Hosea's marital imagery, God chose something that people could understand—human marriage, divorce, and remarriage to illustrate a truth, just as Jesus did when he spoke of sheep and doors to illustrate his own ministry. Those New Testament metaphors work because those aspects of everyday life illustrate Jesus's ministry. And so it is with marital imagery— divorce and remarriage within human marriage relationships illustrate

God's 'divorce' of Israel in the *Divine Marriage*. His people had been unfaithful to him, worshipping other gods, and so he divorces them. And yet, despite the obstacles of Deuteronomy 24, which forbids a wife's return to her original husband, God holds out the hope of a future remarriage.

4.7   God's Divorce in Malachi

Malachi is not generally included in a consideration of Old Testament marital imagery, even though the last twelve books of the Bible, from Hosea to Malachi, can be seen as a unit and are sometimes described as the 'Book of the Twelve.' The first book, Hosea, clearly has a focus on marital imagery, and Malachi, the last book, opens with this statement:

> The oracle of the word of the LORD to Israel by Malachi. "I have loved you," says the LORD… (Malachi 1:1–2)

We know this is addressed to Judah, as Israel (the ten northern tribes) no longer exist at this point in the story; but even after the ten northern tribes were exiled, the Old Testament continues to describe God's people as 'Israel,' although only two tribes (Judah and Benjamin) are left—and when the Old Testament does refer to Judah, it usually means Judah and Benjamin.

Malachi is reminding Judah of God's past love for them. But despite having been brought back from Babylon, Judah still do not seem to have any enthusiasm for the things of God, and many men had married non-Jewish wives.

In Malachi 2:16, as in 2:14 (§3.3), the Hebrew text is very unclear, and some translations suggest that God 'hates divorce'—and this is widely believed to be God giving his view on divorce in human marriage. But we need to consider the context of that statement. As we have seen, Malachi closes the Book of the Twelve, a 'book' that opens with marital imagery—and Malachi's own opening statement is about God's declared love for wayward Judah. Also, God had given a specific *command* to the men of Judah through Ezra (who some think wrote Malachi) to divorce their foreign wives (Ezra 10:11). All these things suggest that God is speaking of his own coming divorce of Judah, and not criticising Jewish men for divorcing their wives. At the close of the book God holds out a promise, but he also gives a warning:

Remember the law of my servant Moses, the statutes and rules that
I commanded him at Horeb for all Israel. Behold, I will send you
Elijah the prophet before the great and awesome day of the LORD
comes. And he will turn the hearts of fathers to their children and
the hearts of children to their fathers, lest I come and strike the land
with a decree of utter destruction. (Malachi 4:4–6)

This perspective sees that the Book of the Twelve opens and closes with
marital imagery portraying the unfaithfulness of God's covenant partner and
the potential consequences of such — a divorce, but this time for Israel's
'sister,' Judah. That divorce duly came. It was pronounced by Jesus (Matthew
23:37–39, Luke 13:34–35) and was symbolised by the destruction of Jerusalem
in 70 CE (see §5.6).

4.8   God's Remarriage

In Hosea

Hosea 1:11 depicts a future reunion of Judah and Israel, and the statement,
'they shall go up from the land' appears to be a prophecy of a future exodus.
And Hosea 2:14–15 follows that same theme, suggesting a journey to a new
promised land — and this time, the 'wilderness' represents not a time of
desolation, but rather a honeymoon, a time of intimacy, devoid of
distractions. Thus, Hosea is saying that the remarriage of God and Israel
involves another exodus — a new exodus — into a new promised land, and vv.
16–23 refer to a new bridal time for God and his people. It is to be a
completely new marriage, a new beginning.

In Isaiah

Isaiah 54 also looks forward to a time of reconciliation. The reference to
Israel's 'widowhood' in v. 4 is probably a reference to Israel's deserted (v. 7),
rather than bereaved, status. Verses 11–17 describe the reconciled Israel as a
rebuilt Jerusalem. In contrast, Isaiah 61:10 speaks of Israel, in the first person
singular, as being dressed like a bridegroom, and like a bride. Isaiah 62:1–8
also seems to refer to a remarriage of God and 'Jerusalem.'

In Jeremiah

Jeremiah 3:18–22 similarly speaks of a reunited nation, and Jeremiah 31:31–32 promises a 'new covenant' which is cited in Hebrews 8:8–13 as being mediated by Christ, who we shall see is portrayed as the 'Bridegroom Messiah' in the Gospels—thus the promise is embraced within the marital imagery of the New Testament.

In Ezekiel

In Ezekiel 40–44 God offers hope for the people, but a new 'bride' is symbolised by a new Jerusalem, the past having been left behind. The new situation is described by Julie Galambush:

> In Ezekiel 33–39, in the aftermath of the Babylonian invasion, the woman Jerusalem is neither condemned nor forgiven, but forgotten. The only remnant of Yahweh's former wife is the abiding memory of her uncleanness. Ezekiel's vision in chaps 40–48 of the new temple city completes the cycle of the city's defilement, destruction, and restoration. The God who left in rage returns in triumph, and the city is renewed and recreated.[25]

4.9   God's Marriage has Asymmetrical Responsibilities

God's 'marriage' to Adam, and then to Israel, is portrayed as having asymmetrical responsibilities—in other words, the partners in the marriage have different duties. This should not surprise us, as the source domain of the imagery, human marriage, also had different gender-based responsibilities, and it is that source domain that populated the target domain.

God provided Adam with everything he needed, he even clothed Adam and Eve after the Fall. And similarly, he provided Israel with food and water in the desert, and a home in the promised land. In return Israel had to keep God's commands—but it is to be noted that in the end, Israel was only sent away because she went with other gods.

We have seen in §3.3 that human marriage was volitional in its formation. And so it is in the *Divine Marriage*. Israel was invited in to the covenant with

God, never compelled. In Egypt, all the people of Israel were invited to prepare the Passover and to daube the blood on their doorposts to protect themselves from the angel of death and partake in the Exodus.

Nor was Israel ever compelled to stay in their relationship with God. In Joshua 24, many years after Sinai, Joshua gathered all Israel together at Shechem and pleaded with them to put away their false gods and be faithful to the one true God. Verse 15 explains that Joshua said they had to 'choose this day whom you will serve.' Even though God had fully provided for her, if she chose, she could go. Once having made this commitment, even then Israel was not compelled to take up the offer of the promised land— Numbers 32 tells how Reuben and Gad chose to settle east of Jordan.

Thus God acts towards Israel, his 'wife' in the Bible's marital imagery, precisely in accord with his own given marriage law in Exodus 21:10–11. Those verses teach that a husband must provide for his wife, and yet not compel her to stay in the relationship. We can now map the Old Testament *Divine Marriage* of God and Israel in the Old Testament with some associated Bible references:

MAP 4 GOD IS THE HUSBAND OF ISRAEL

SOURCE DOMAIN	TARGET DOMAIN
HUMAN MARRIAGE	**GOD IS THE HUSBAND OF ISRAEL**
A woman becomes the wife of a man in a new family union formed by means of a marriage covenant. (Genesis 2:24)	Israel becomes the 'wife' of God by means of a marriage covenant. (Jeremiah 31:31–32)

ROOT METAPHOR

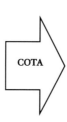

COTA

• Marital obligations for the husband (Exodus 21:7–11) • Adultery forbidden (Exodus 20:14) • Divorce certificate required (Deuteronomy 24:1–4) • Remarriage to first husband forbidden (Deuteronomy 24:1–4)	• Marital obligations for God (Psalm 132:13–16) • Adultery forbidden (Ezekiel 23:1–9) • Divorce certificate required (Jeremiah 3:6–8) • Remarriage to God forbidden (Jeremiah 3:6–8) • But a future betrothal followed by a remarriage is promised (Hosea 2:19–20; Isaiah 54:4–8)

COTA = Consequent Old Testament Analogies

4.10   Summary

It was suggested in §4.1 that if we study God's own 'marriage' we can learn something about what God thought a marriage should be like. We have seen that the Sinaitic covenant (God's 'marriage' to Israel) is an asymmetrical, contractual, volitional, conditional relationship. This mirrors, as metaphor theory would lead us to expect, human marriage as portrayed in the Old Testament narratives and legislated for in the Pentateuch.

In other words, God's marriage to Israel was a Genesis 2:24 marriage. No aspect of Adam and Eve's marriage is used anywhere in the Old Testament to describe either the *Divine Marriage* or human marriage.

Some key points

1. God describes his relationship with Israel as a Genesis 2:24 marriage, no features of Adam and Eve's marriage are used to illustrate that *Divine Marriage*.

2. The Bible says that our holy God divorced Israel and separated from Judah.

3. At every point, divorce and remarriage in the *Divine Marriage* is in accord with God's rules for human marriage as recorded in the Bible.

4. God promises a future reconciliation, a remarriage, for a new united nation.

Some questions

1. Our holy God divorced Israel—should that impact our understanding of divorce?

2. For God to offer a remarriage to Israel appears to contradict his own rule in Deuteronomy 24—can you suggest how he was going to circumvent that rule?

3. Do you think God thought that human marriage happened to be an ideal vehicle to illustrate his own relationship with his people, or did God intentionally give, and design marriage from the beginning for this purpose?

Chapter 5: Jesus the Bridegroom of the Church

5.1 Introduction

We have seen in chapter 4 that the Old Testament marital imagery tells the story of God in a covenantal relationship with Adam that resembled a marriage, and of Adam being sent away from the garden taking all mankind with him. We saw that God entered a new covenantal relationship with Israel at Sinai and that this is specifically described by Jeremiah as a marriage. But eventually the ten northern tribes were taken away by Assyria, both Isaiah and Jeremiah describing that as a divorce from God. The marital imagery makes it clear that it was a divorce brought about because of Israel's pursuit of 'other gods,' in other words, a lack of faithfulness to God, more than any lack of obedience to the many laws associated with the Sinaitic covenant.

Judah was spared that Assyrian exile, but even she was eventually sent away to Babylon for the same reason. It was there that she wept with regret over her seemingly hopeless situation. However, God eventually brought Judah back home to Palestine. Despite this, the Old Testament closed with a warning, in Malachi chapter 4, that unless Judah changed her ways she would suffer a dreadful fate.

But throughout the Old Testament marital imagery, in Hosea, Isaiah, Jeremiah, and Ezekiel, there is a promise of a future remarriage. For example, in Jeremiah 31:

> Behold, the days are coming, declares the LORD, when I will make a new covenant with the house of Israel and the house of Judah, not like the covenant that I made with their fathers on the day when I took them by the hand to bring them out of the land of Egypt, my covenant that they broke, though I was their husband, declares the LORD. But this is the covenant that I will make with the house of Israel after those days, declares the LORD: I will put my law within them, and I will write it on their hearts. And I will be their God, and they shall be my people. (Jeremiah 31:31–33)

Nobody was sure at the time what these remarriage prophecies meant in practice, but in the 400 years between the close of the Old Testament and the beginning of the New Testament, there was a heightened expectancy that God was about to do something. It was at this time that Jesus was born, and at the beginning of his ministry, John the Baptist declared of him:

> You yourselves bear me witness, that I said, "I am not the Christ, but I have been sent before him." The one who has the bride is the bridegroom. The friend of the bridegroom, who stands and hears him, rejoices greatly at the bridegroom's voice. Therefore this joy of mine is now complete. (John 3:28–29)

In chapter 4 we looked at Old Testament marital imagery to understand how God thinks a human marriage should work. In this chapter, we will look at New Testament imagery with that same aim in mind. We will see that Jesus, the Bridegroom Messiah, God incarnate, invites unredeemed humanity ('divorced' at Eden because of Adam's sin), divorced Israel, and separated Judah, to the marriage supper of the Lamb. In other words, all alive at the time of Jesus (or since) who identified with any of these people groups, Jew or Gentile, could come to him in a new marriage.

This imagery explains some of the reasons why Jesus had to die—the elect (the church) is 'washed in the blood of the Lamb' so that she can be deemed a virgin bride. This was to fulfil the Old Testament law which said a high priest (as Jesus is to believers) must marry a virgin (Leviticus 21:10–14; Hebrews 9:11)—this is the new beginning that Hosea prophesied (§4.8). The marital history of the various people groups represented in the new bridal community is wiped clean. Jesus's death also circumvents the Deuteronomy 24 rule that would have prevented him, God in the flesh, marrying the 'wife' (Jew and Gentile) he had divorced.

What is more, Jewish bridegrooms paid a *mohar* (bride-price) to the bride's father—it was their pledge to return and take her to their own home. As he approached his death, Jesus prayed to God the father, 'I glorified you on earth, having accomplished the work that you gave me to do' (John 17:4). His death was the *mohar* for his bride, the church, his pledge to her heavenly father that he would return and take her to his heavenly home.

When we look at what Christ's death achieved on the cross from the perspective of the Bible's marital imagery, it is like looking at a multifaceted diamond caught in the light, shining brilliantly in many directions at once. However, to explore such is beyond the scope of this book. What is more, there are so many New Testament passages that allude to the *Divine Marriage* that I am only able to select a few to fulfil the remit of this chapter, which is to look at how Jesus's mission is portrayed as a bridegroom, inviting humanity 'divorced' when Adam was ejected from Eden (a fallen humanity that includes divorced Israel), to the marriage supper of the Lamb. But from those selected it will be seen that the New Testament writers systematically exploit contemporary Jewish marital practices to illustrate and inform us about Jesus's ministry.

5.2   The Wedding at Cana

In John 2:1–11, when at the wedding in Cana, Mary commented to Jesus on the shortfall of wine. It seems that at Jewish weddings it was the bridegroom's responsibility to provide the wine (as inferred in v. 9). This probably accounts for Jesus's reply to her, 'Woman, what does this have to do with me? My hour is not yet come' (v .4). Mary had been, in effect, asking Jesus to prematurely declare himself as the messianic bridegroom. However, a short time later Jesus declares to the Samaritan woman, 'But the hour is coming, and is now here, when the true worshipers will worship the Father in spirit and truth, for the Father is seeking such people to worship him.'

Despite his comment at Cana, Jesus nonetheless did as his mother had requested and performed the miracle. When the wine is produced, the master of the feast comments on its quality and assumes it is the bridegroom who has made the provision (vv. 9–10). Many of the readers of John's Gospel would know the book of Isaiah very well and would not have missed the significance of this miracle. Isaiah 24:7, 9, 11 probably refers to a lack of wine when Israel was suffering from the Assyrian invasion. But then in the very next chapter Isaiah describes a future restoration when God will ensure wine will be in abundance (Isaiah 25:6–8).

Isaiah said it was God who was going to provide, 'a feast of well-aged wine'—now Jesus had done exactly that. It seems clear that Jesus is showing the wedding guests, and through John showing us, that he is God in the flesh, come as the promised Bridegroom Messiah, and that the time for the promised restoration, and a new start, had at last come.

5.3   The Bridegroom Introduced

We have seen how in John 3:22–30 Jesus is introduced as the bridegroom and John the Baptist describes his joy at hearing the 'bridegroom's voice,' which is almost certainly a reference to Jeremiah 33:10–11, 14–17—verses that speak of God restoring Judah when, as Jeremiah explains, the voice of a bridegroom will be heard. So again, John is using marital imagery to identify Jesus as both Bridegroom Messiah and Davidic king. And when John the Baptist describes himself as the 'friend of the bridegroom,' he is in effect comparing his role to that of the best man in a Jewish wedding, whose duty was to lead the bride to the bridegroom when the time for the wedding had arrived.

5.4   The Woman from Samaria

In John 4:1–29 we have the story of the woman from Samaria. The first ten verses set the scene:

> Now when Jesus learned that the Pharisees had heard that Jesus was making and baptizing more disciples than John (although Jesus himself did not baptize, but only his disciples), he left Judea and departed again for Galilee. And he had to pass through Samaria. So he came to a town of Samaria called Sychar, near the field that Jacob had given to his son Joseph. Jacob's well was there; so Jesus, wearied as he was from his journey, was sitting beside the well. It was about the sixth hour.
>
> There a woman from Samaria came to draw water. Jesus said to her, "Give me a drink." (For his disciples had gone away into the city to buy food.) The Samaritan woman said to him, "How is it that you, a Jew, ask for a drink from me, a woman of Samaria?" (For Jews have no dealings with Samaritans.) Jesus answered her, "If you knew the gift of God, and who it is that is saying to you, 'Give me a drink,' you would have asked him, and he would have given you living water." (John 4:1–10)

I suggest in this encounter that Jesus is treating this woman not just as an individual, but as a symbol for her people, and presenting himself as a bridegroom and offering to her a 'marriage'—in other words, inviting both her, and the despised Samaritans, to come to God.

There are clear connections in this story with previous meetings at a well that resulted in marriage (Isaac and Rebekah, Genesis 24:14–16; Jacob and Rachel, Genesis 29:1–20; Moses and Zipporah, Exodus 2:15–17, 21). It is an example of the New Testament alluding to another event, as was discussed in §1.5. It will be remembered that it was pointed out that there are several criteria employed by Bible exegetes to detect such allusions, and this passage in John 4 fulfils virtually all of them. There are so many detailed parallels (particularly with Jacob and Rachel's meeting at a well recorded in Genesis 29) that only a few can be mentioned. For example, John portrays Jesus, just like Jacob, as a man from another a country, seeking a bride, arriving at a well at the middle of the day, and asking a single woman for a drink, who on realising the man's identity, ran home to tell her people. What is more, Jacob is specifically referenced no fewer than three times in the account in John 4.

We will confine ourselves to just a few aspects of the passage to try to see something of the significance of this woman's encounter with Jesus, and in turn gain further insight into divorce and remarriage in the *Divine Marriage*. In v. 10 Jesus says, 'If you knew the gift of God, and who it is that is saying to you, "Give me a drink," you would have asked him, and he would have given you living water.' Jesus turns the conversation from literal water to spiritual matters, the term 'living water' here almost certainly carrying the same deeper meaning as it does in John 7:

> On the last day of the feast, the great day, Jesus stood up and cried out, "If anyone thirsts, let him come to me and drink. Whoever believes in me, as the Scripture has said, 'Out of his heart will flow rivers of living water." Now this he said about the Spirit, whom those who believed in him were to receive, for as yet the Spirit had not been given, because Jesus was not yet glorified. (John 7:37–39)

But in his conversation with the Samaritan woman, Jesus's reference to living water may have an additional meaning. There is evidence that 'living water' had bridal associations—referring to the ritual bath a Jewish bride took before her wedding.[26] Indeed, in the Old Testament, in the Song of Solomon 4:12, 15, there is a link with a bride and living water: 'A garden locked is my sister, my bride, a spring locked, a fountain sealed … a garden fountain, a well of living water.' Furthermore, some see that Jesus's reference to 'the gift of God' (v. 10) is an allusion to the gifts that Isaac gave to Rebekah at their first meeting by a well (Genesis 24:22–27). It seems that with these allusions Jesus is drawing the woman into an understanding of his identity as the Bridegroom Messiah.

It might be thought that the passage would never have been understood this way by the Samaritan woman, or by any readers of John's account at the time he wrote it. But I think it can be demonstrated that the Samaritan woman did indeed understand what Jesus was saying, and that it is likely that the contemporary readers would have done so as well.

Firstly, we should consider the context of this story in John's Gospel: in chapter 2 there is the wedding at Cana, then in chapter 3 John the Baptist specifically calls Jesus the bridegroom, and now chapter 4 relates this encounter. Secondly, I believe the location of the encounter is significant. In first century Palestine, there was no internet dating. If a young man wanted to meet a young woman the well was the best place to go—as we have mentioned, Moses, Isaac, and Jacob all met their wives there. Jesus, a single man, was alone with this woman, a place where you go to meet a potential marriage partner, and this might explain the reaction of the disciples when they came back and found him there (v. 27).

Thirdly, it is Jesus himself who introduces the marital theme when he asks her to bring her husband (vv. 16–18). Some think Jesus wants to point out the woman's dubious marital history, but this does not fit the redemptive theme of the encounter. Furthermore, notwithstanding her latest relationship, there is no teaching in the Jewish Scriptures that to have had five husbands was in any way sinful. Marriage after divorce or the death of a husband was normal in those times, in fact it was often necessary if a woman was to survive financially. Even in England in the 16th century when a Roman Catholic sacramental view of marriage prevailed, Catherine Parr, the last wife of Henry VIII, was married four times, and yet widely perceived as a pious woman.

Fourthly, not just the location, but the religious context also supports an interpretation that a wider issue was being addressed. The Samaritan people were the remnants of the northern tribes of Israel that had been 'divorced' by God—Samaria had been the home of Ephraim when the Assyrians invaded; some had stayed, but others were deported to Assyria. Although many subsequently returned, in the process there had been much intermarrying with foreigners—the Samaritans were now a mixture of Jewish and Gentile blood and no longer considered 'Jewish' by their Jewish neighbours. What is more, they embraced a religion that was a mixture of Judaism and idolatry. They worshipped the true God, but they also had a history of involvement with the cults of five different nations—these were referred to as the five false gods of Samaria, as demonstrated by Josephus in his writings.[27] The Canaanite word for a god is *Baal*, the same word sometimes used for 'husband' in the Hebrew Bible (Hosea making a wordplay on it in Hosea 2:16). The fact that the Samaritans worshipped the true God, but also had a history of worshipping these five false gods, was well known. The Old Testament account of them is found in 2 Kings 17:24–34. Verses 33–34 summarise the situation:

> So they feared the LORD but also served their own gods, after the manner of the nations from among whom they had been carried away. To this day they do according to the former manner. They do not fear the LORD, and they do not follow the statutes or the rules or the law or the commandment that the LORD commanded the children of Jacob, whom he named Israel.

The Samaritans had an outward appearance of 'fearing the LORD' in their worship, but in reality, they did not fear him at all as they did not keep his commands. Thus the Jews looked down on them because of their mixed blood, their false gods, and the fact they had their own temple on Mount Gerizim which, however, the Samaritans insisted was designated by Moses as the place where the nation should worship. In summary, there were two issues relating to their worship—the five false gods, and the true God the Samaritans worshipped, but at the wrong temple.

I suggest that all these things are key to Jesus's conversation with this woman at the well. Jesus was steadily moving to the point he wanted to make—he is the Messiah, the Saviour of Jew, Gentile, and even of the Samaritans. He is the Christ who is going to sweep away the idea that God could only be worshipped in one particular place. Jesus points to her five husbands (five false gods), and the fact that the man she is presently co-habiting with is not her husband. This last relationship was wrong, and thus an analogy automatically arises from this sixth 'husband,' to the Samaritan worship of the true God (the sixth 'god'), but at the wrong temple.

If we look at the relevant section from our passage in John 4, vv. 16–20, most commentators say that the woman at this point changes the topic to speak of religious things so as to divert Jesus away from her private life. But the woman, I believe, makes it clear that she had understood exactly what Jesus was saying. In her reply to him at v. 19, immediately after acknowledging Jesus's supernatural knowledge of her private life ('Sir, I perceive that you are a prophet'), goes directly to speak of that temple (her sixth 'god'): 'Our fathers worshiped on this mountain, but you say that in Jerusalem is the place where people ought to worship.' Jesus, the master evangelist, with the illustration from her private life, had brought her to the precise point he wanted—to show that now the promised Christ had come, and the temples at Gerizim and Jerusalem were of no consequence, clearly implying the end of the Jew/Gentile division as Jesus explains in vv. 21–26.

In this conversation with Jesus, the woman is serving as a symbol for lost Israel, just as had Hosea's wife, Gomer, in a previous century. I believe that Jesus is offering the woman, and through her, the Samaritan people (divorced Israel), in this traditional Jewish setting for betrothals, redemption in a new marriage. The Roman Catholic scholar, Brant Pitre, says:

> through this encounter with Jesus the non-Jewish peoples of the world begin to be betrothed—so to speak—to the one who is both Bridegroom Messiah and Savior of the world.[28]

Verses 28–29 of John 4 tell us:

> So the woman left her water jar and went away into town and said to the people, "Come, see a man who told me all that I ever did. Can this be the Christ?"

It seems that the woman had again realised the significance of what Jesus had said, and went to tell not her family, or her household, but 'the people.' Who were 'the people'? They were the Samaritans. But tell them what? Her

focus was not her personal salvation. She said, as the New American
Standard Bible has it, 'Come, see a man who told me all the things that I have
done.' She was amazed at Jesus's prophetic knowledge, but I suggest even
more than that, she was amazed by his declaration of the abolition of the
Jew/Gentile division. Could it be that the gist of her message was: 'Can this
be the Christ? If so, can it be that he has come for us, even us, whom the Jews
despise?'

We can see that this encounter between Jesus and the Samaritan woman
recorded by John is fully in keeping with the Old Testament marital imagery,
Calum Carmichael commenting on John's 'consummate mastery' of both the
story and the imagery.[29]

Hosea, Isaiah, Jeremiah, and Ezekiel all prophesy a better future for Israel,
and such is often described as a remarriage:

> For your Maker is your husband, the LORD of hosts is his name; and
> the Holy One of Israel is your Redeemer, the God of the whole earth
> he is called. For the LORD has called you like a wife deserted and
> grieved in spirit, like a wife of youth when she is cast off, says your
> God. For a brief moment I deserted you, but with great compassion
> I will gather you. (Isaiah 54:5–7)

Isaiah is telling us that it is God himself who will come for Israel and be the
husband. And Hosea specifically says that this future involves both Israel
(now the Samaritans) and Judah:

> Yet the number of the children of Israel shall be like the sand of the
> sea, which cannot be measured or numbered. And in the place where
> it was said to them, "You are not my people," it shall be said to them,
> "Children of the living God." And the children of Judah and the
> children of Israel shall be gathered together, and they shall appoint
> for themselves one head. And they shall go up from the land, for
> great shall be the day of Jezreel. (Hosea 1:10–11)

'Jezreel' is another wordplay by Hosea (as in Hosea 2:16)—in Hebrew it looks
and sounds just like 'Israel.' It was God who had married Israel, God who

had divorced her, and it is the same God who promises a remarriage—it is a glorious future for 'Jezreel.'

We can see from this encounter with the Samaritan woman that Jesus does not speak as a messenger. He does not say to her: 'Go to God, he is ready to be reconciled to you, and to your people, in fulfilment of his long-promised remarriage.' Instead Jesus says to her, and to others in the Gospel narratives, come to *me*. Many theologians since the 19th century have suggested that the church after the New Testament era read the divinity of Christ back into the New Testament, and that Jesus himself did not think he was God. But the Gospel writers portray Jesus in his ministry as self-consciously taking on the role of the Bridegroom Messiah, and this imagery is tightly bound into the Gospel story—it could not be a later addition.

5.5   Jesus's Ministry is the Betrothal Period

As suggested above, the account in John 4 portraying Jesus as a bridegroom is not an isolated example—all the Gospel writers use several contemporary marriage customs involving a bridegroom to describe Jesus's earthly ministry as a betrothal period. For example, when he was asked why his disciples were not fasting, Jesus answered:

> Can the wedding guests fast while the bridegroom is with them? As long as they have the bridegroom with them, they cannot fast. The days will come when the bridegroom is taken away from them, and then they will fast in that day. (Mark 2:19–20)

'Wedding guests' in the original Greek are actually 'sons of the bride chamber' and contemporary records show that these were special friends of the bridegroom excused from religious duties for the wedding week celebration. Jesus is describing his period of ministry before his death on the cross as if it were the week the bridegroom has preparing for his wedding.

Jewish weddings climaxed not with the arrival of the bride at the church, but with the arrival of the bridegroom at the wedding feast, where he would be met by the bridesmaids. Thus, the parable of the ten virgins in Matthew 25:1–13 is based on what happened at contemporary weddings—except that Jesus in the story arrives when he was not expected. After the wedding, the groom would take his bride to the marital home he had prepared for her.

Jesus reassures us that he has prepared a home for believers:

> Let not your hearts be troubled. Believe in God; believe also in me. In my Father's house are many rooms. If it were not so, would I have told you that I go to prepare a place for you? And if I go and prepare a place for you, I will come again and will take you to myself, that where I am you may be also. (John 14:1–3)

At the wedding at Cana when Jesus said, 'My hour has not yet come,' I suggested Jesus was referring to the beginning of his earthly ministry (also John 4:23; 5:25). But in John 13:1, Jesus's hour is associated not with the beginning of his ministry, but the end. We read, 'Now before the Feast of the Passover, when Jesus knew that his hour had come to depart out of this world to the Father....' The Gospels (for example Luke 22:14–23) describe the situation, and 1 Corinthians 11:25 says:

> In the same way also he took the cup, after supper, saying, "This cup is the new covenant in my blood. Do this, as often as you drink it, in remembrance of me."

Thus, the Last Supper is linked to the new marriage covenant promised by God to Israel in Jeremiah 31:31–33. In effect, the Last Supper is Jesus's own wedding banquet, and the twelve disciples represent Jesus's bride, the church.

Paul tells us in 1 Corinthians 6:

> Or do you not know that your body is a temple of the Holy Spirit within you, whom you have from God? You are not your own, for you were bought with a price. So glorify God in your body. (1 Corinthians 6:19–20)

In v. 19 the Greek 'your' is plural and 'body' is singular, thus making it clear that it is the church collectively that is the temple of the Holy Spirit, the body of Christ raised up to replace the Jerusalem temple, John 2:19 telling us that Jesus said: 'Destroy this temple, and in three days I will raise it up.' So Paul says that 'you [the church] were bought with a price.' It is Jesus, the divine bridegroom, who pays the *mohar* for his bride. Hosea, uniquely in the Old Testament marital imagery, speaks of a future betrothal for God's people:

> And I will betroth you to me forever. I will betroth you to me in righteousness and in justice, in steadfast love and in mercy. I will betroth you to me in faithfulness. And you shall know the LORD. (Hosea 2:19–20)

Then, in chapter 3, God speaks again through Hosea, whose wayward wife Gomer is a symbol of Israel, and tells us that the new marriage is to be preceded by a betrothal period—and it is a betrothal with a *mohar* ('fifteen shekels of silver and a homer and a lethech of barley'):

> And the LORD said to me, "Go again, love a woman who is loved by another man and is an adulteress, even as the LORD loves the children of Israel, though they turn to other gods and love cakes of raisins." So I bought her for fifteen shekels of silver and a homer and a lethech of barley. And I said to her, "You must dwell as mine for many days. You shall not play the whore, or belong to another man; so will I also be to you." For the children of Israel shall dwell many days without king or prince, without sacrifice or pillar, without ephod or household gods. Afterwards the children of Israel shall return and seek the LORD their God, and David their king, and they shall come in fear to the LORD and to his goodness in the latter days. (Hosea 3)

A virgin can certainly expect a *mohar*, but it would be unusual to give one for a woman of low repute such as Gomer—yet, as mentioned above (§5.1), Jesus has washed the church clean with his blood. And so, with his death on the cross, Christ also pays the *mohar* for his church, and the betrothal period begins—it will end when he comes for his bride. During this betrothal time (Hosea's prophecy calls it the 'latter days') many Jews will turn in faith to 'David their king' (Hosea 3:5)—that is, the Lord Jesus Christ.

Paul's comment in 2 Corinthians 11:2 refers to this time, 'For I feel a divine jealousy for you, for I betrothed you to one husband, to present you as a pure virgin to Christ'—it was the responsibility of the bride's father, having received the *mohar*, to ensure his daughter remained a virgin as she awaited her bridegroom. And so Jesus goes to the cross to secure his bride as prophesied. And even here, the marital imagery does not end. All Jewish bridegrooms wore a seamless robe and a crown on their wedding day (Exodus 28:31–32 cf. Isaiah 61:10; Song 3:11)—just as Jesus wore on the day of his crucifixion (Matthew 27:27–29; John 19:23). This symbolism on the cross is a pre-echo of the marriage supper of the Lamb at the end of time.

2 Timothy describes the situation as we await Jesus's return:

> Therefore I endure everything for the sake of the elect, that they also may obtain the salvation that is in Christ Jesus with eternal glory. The saying is trustworthy, for: If we have died with him, we will also live with him; if we endure, we will also reign with him; if we deny him, he also will deny us; if we are faithless, he remains faithful— for he cannot deny himself. (2 Timothy 2:10–13)

The bridegroom would be honour-bound to come for his bride having promised her father and paid the *mohar* to seal the arrangement—only her sexual unfaithfulness could justify him breaking that promise. Thus Joseph was described as a just man even though he sought to break their betrothal and 'divorce' Mary because of her presumed sexual unfaithfulness (Matthew 1:18–19).

Paul is saying here in 2 Timothy 2 that even if Christian believers give up hope that Jesus would ever come for them he would still honour his promise. Only if we 'deny him,' only if we walk away from him and choose another, will he deny us. Many Christians rightly hold to the view that true believers are secure with Christ, but those in the visible church that have a false profession will be lost, as Jesus explains in Matthew 7:21–23.

The church's betrothal period finally ends when, in Revelation chapter 19, Christ appears at the end of time and celebrates with the church, his bride, the marriage supper of the Lamb.

5.6   Jesus's Divorce of Judah

Judah was not divorced by God, but nonetheless, she was sent away to Babylon, although eventually she was brought back to Palestine. However, as we have seen, the closing verses of Malachi contain this warning from God:

> Remember the law of my servant Moses, the statutes and rules that I commanded him at Horeb for all Israel. Behold, I will send you Elijah the prophet before the great and awesome day of the LORD comes. And he will turn the hearts of fathers to their children and the hearts of children to their fathers, lest I come and strike the land with a decree of utter destruction. (Malachi 4:4–6)

These words form the last words of our Old Testament. So Malachi was promising Elijah as a final messenger, and Matthew sees this person as being represented by John the Baptist (despite his claim otherwise—Matthew 11:10–14 cf. John 1:21).[30] We know that Jerusalem was destroyed in 70 CE, and that Jesus prophesied this in Matthew 23 (also Luke 13:34–35):

> O Jerusalem, Jerusalem, the city that kills the prophets and stones those who are sent to it! How often would I have gathered your children together as a hen gathers her brood under her wings, and you would not! See, your house is left to you desolate. For I tell you, you will not see me again, until you say, "Blessed is he who comes in the name of the Lord." (Matthew 23:37–39)

It seems that the comment, 'See, your house is left to you desolate' is a fulfilment of Malachi's warning of 'utter destruction.' Although the predominant feature of the marital imagery in the New Testament is that Jesus is the bridegroom, in this divorce of Judah he acted in a different capacity—that of the husband, God the Father, divorcing the people he had taken to himself at Sinai. And thus it is Jesus who finally cancels that covenant with a divorce. The situation is explained in Hebrews 8:6–13. In vv. 8–12 the writer cites Jeremiah 31:31–34 where we are told of the promised new marriage, the new covenant that replaces the old covenant:

> But as it is, Christ has obtained a ministry that is as much more excellent than the old as the covenant he mediates is better, since it is enacted on better promises. For if that first covenant had been faultless, there would have been no occasion to look for a second. For he finds fault with them when he says: "Behold, the days are

coming, declares the Lord, when I will establish a new covenant with the house of Israel and with the house of Judah, not like the covenant that I made with their fathers on the day when I took them by the hand to bring them out of the land of Egypt. For they did not continue in my covenant, and so I showed no concern for them, declares the Lord. For this is the covenant that I will make with the house of Israel after those days, declares the Lord: I will put my laws into their minds, and write them on their hearts, and I will be their God, and they shall be my people. And they shall not teach, each one his neighbour and each one his brother, saying, 'Know the Lord,' for they shall all know me, from the least of them to the greatest. For I will be merciful toward their iniquities, and I will remember their sins no more." In speaking of a new covenant, he makes the first one obsolete. And what is becoming obsolete and growing old is ready to vanish away. (Hebrews 8:6–13)

It is thought Hebrews was written in c. 65 CE, and we are told in v. 13 that the old covenant is 'ready to vanish away'—and finally does when the temple, the centre of the nation's religious life, is raised to the ground in the destruction of Jerusalem in 70 CE. The divorce Jesus promised in Matthew 23 and Luke 13 was finally enacted. The temple is never rebuilt, even to this day.

5.7   The Marriage Supper of the Lamb

The focus of the Book of Revelation is on the consummation of the *Divine Marriage*, and so, unlike the Gospels, where Jesus was acting out the role of a bridegroom preparing for his wedding day, in Revelation there are very few references to Jewish wedding customs. However, the very title of the book, derived from its first verse, 'The revelation of Jesus Christ ...' is perhaps a reflection of the ancient Jewish custom of the bridegroom lifting the veil covering his bride's face. And at the climax of the book we are told that the 'marriage of the Lamb has come, and his bride has made herself ready' (Revelation 19:6)—the bridegroom coming to collect his bride in the tradition of Jewish weddings. The bride is the church, the elect, that is any who turn by faith to Christ. The bride consists of both Jews and Gentiles— the two people groups who form all humanity, whom God has said he had 'divorced' (Genesis 3:23–24; Jeremiah 3:1–8). And the bridegroom? It is the Lord Jesus Christ, who had declared his divorce of Judah. Both bride and groom are divorcees.

5.8   A Metanarrative

The Bible's marital imagery is its overarching story, or we might say its 'metanarrative.' Although God 'divorces' Adam and his progeny in the Garden of Eden, he makes a fresh start with Israel and a new marriage at Sinai, but then he divorces Israel for her idolatry. Later, he sends Judah away to Babylon for the same reason, but subsequently, brings her back to Palestine.

However, Judah knew that their return to Palestine was not the glorious remarriage that the prophets had spoken of. Instead it was a dispirited nation that made half-hearted attempts to rebuild the temple—and all the while they were ruled by foreign nations. They were in effect captives in their own land. This is the background to one of Jesus's first proclamations of the purpose of his ministry, when immediately after his 40 days fasting in the desert we are told:

> And he came to Nazareth, where he had been brought up. And as was his custom, he went to the synagogue on the Sabbath day, and he stood up to read. And the scroll of the prophet Isaiah was given to him. He unrolled the scroll and found the place where it was written, "The Spirit of the Lord is upon me, because he has anointed me to proclaim good news to the poor. He has sent me to proclaim liberty to the captives and recovering of sight to the blind, to set at liberty those who are oppressed, to proclaim the year of the Lord's favour." And he rolled up the scroll and gave it back to the attendant and sat down. And the eyes of all in the synagogue were fixed on him. And he began to say to them, "Today this Scripture has been fulfilled in your hearing." (Luke 4:16–21)

As a young Christian I was somewhat puzzled by this declaration by Jesus, 'proclaim liberty to the captives and recovering of sight to the blind, to set at liberty those who are oppressed, to proclaim the year of the Lord's favour'— it did not seem to fit what I had been told. I thought Jesus had come to say that all who believed in him would have eternal life. However, Jesus is reading from Isaiah 61 which foretold the day, or so it was thought at the time, when Judah would be freed from their captivity in Babylon. The chapter goes on to say:

> to grant to those who mourn in Zion—to give them a beautiful headdress instead of ashes, the oil of gladness instead of mourning, the garment of praise instead of a faint spirit; that they may be called oaks of righteousness, the planting of the LORD, that he may be glorified. They shall build up the ancient ruins; they shall raise up the former devastations; they shall repair the ruined cities, the devastations of many generations. (Isaiah 61:3–4)

This is more than a trek back from Babylon, it is God promising his people a glorious future. Verse 10 says:

> I will greatly rejoice in the LORD; my soul shall exult in my God, for he has clothed me with the garments of salvation; he has covered me with the robe of righteousness, as a bridegroom decks himself like a priest with a beautiful headdress, and as a bride adorns herself with her jewels.

Jesus, when he stood in the synagogue that day and said, 'Today this Scripture has been fulfilled in your hearing'—was clearly saying that he was that bridegroom, who had come to offer to Judah, and any that would hear and believe, a completely new 'marriage'—a new covenant. Thus Jesus was linking his ministry with the exodus and freedom from captivity that Isaiah promised.

In the last sixty years or so, many scholars have seen that this theme runs through much of the New Testament—it is an area of study called 'new exodus' theology. Moses was a man chosen by God to lead an exodus to the 'marriage' at Sinai. That exodus began with the death of a lamb in each household. For those that believed God's promise and daubed the blood on the doorposts, the angel of death passed over them. But Jesus, although leading an exodus to a marriage as Moses did, is not like Moses. This time God has not sent a messenger, he has come himself to claim his bride, and as God incarnate, the Lamb of God, he dies for us on the cross at Passover time.

This is the beginning of the new exodus God had promised. It is not a dispirited journey from Babylon back to a Palestine dominated by the Romans. Instead the Bridegroom Messiah leads his bridal community, the elect of God, on an exodus to a new heavens and earth.

It is possible to 'map' the New Testament marital imagery like this:

MAP 5 JESUS IS THE BRIDEGROOM OF THE CHURCH

SOURCE DOMAIN		TARGET DOMAIN
Human Marriage		**JESUS IS THE BRIDEGROOM OF THE CHURCH**
A woman becomes the wife of a man in a new family union formed by means of the marriage covenant. (Genesis 2:24)	ROOT METAPHOR →	Men and women are invited to become members of the covenant community that is the metaphoric bride of Christ.

• Betrothal (Matthew 1:18)		• Betrothal (2 Corinthians 11:2)
• Wedding feast		• Wedding feast (Matthew 22:1–14)
• Invitations to guests		• Invitations to guests (John 4:5–29)
• Groom prepares a place for his bride		• Jesus prepares a place for the church (John 14:1–3)
• Groom pays a *mohar* for his bride	CNTA →	• Jesus pays a *mohar* for the church (1 Corinthians 6:19–20)
• Groom promises to care for his bride		• Christ cares for the church (Ephesians 5:22–29)
• Bride waits for groom		• The church waits for Jesus (2 Timothy 2:10–13)
• Groom comes for his bride		• Jesus comes for the church (Matthew 25:1–13)
• Groom takes his bride to his own home		• Jesus takes the church to his own home (Revelation 21:1–4)

CNTA = Consequent New Testament Analogies

5.9   Summary

The Old Testament marital imagery, which began in the Garden of Eden, and culminated with the threat of a divorce of Judah in Malachi, continues seamlessly into the New Testament. The promised Messiah, Jesus Christ, steps on to the stage of history with John the Baptist's declaration that he is the bridegroom. The New Testament progressively reveals the truth of this statement. Jesus is not a messenger telling people to go to God for forgiveness and get ready for a new marriage to him—instead, he says come to me. He was declaring himself to be that husband, God in the flesh, come to make good on the Old Testament promises of a new marriage. Anybody that wanted to come to him—Jew or Gentile—could be there at the great wedding supper at the end of time.

This portrayal of Jesus's ministry as the Bridegroom Messiah in the New Testament is entirely consonant with God's marriage with Israel, in that it represents an asymmetrical, volitional, conditional, covenant. Jesus takes upon himself the human bridegroom's role. He prepares and offers his bridal community a new home. It is a *volitional* offer—none are forced to come to Christ against their will. We can come based on the *condition* that we believe on him and have no other gods.

All the New Testament betrothal imagery is rooted in the understanding of a Genesis 2:24 human marriage, consonant with the understanding of human marriage and that of the marital imagery in the Old Testament. As in the Old Testament marital imagery, so in the New Testament betrothal imagery, no aspect of the primal couple marriage is employed.

We can now turn to the New Testament to see how it uses Genesis 2:24 in its teaching about human marriage and divorce.

Some key points

1. The New Testament picks up the Old Testament marital imagery and presents Jesus as the Bridegroom Messiah who has come to fulfil the Old Testament promises of a remarriage.

2. Jesus invites his people on a new exodus from this world to the next.

3. All are invited to join him, whatever their personal history or ethnic origin.

4. All at the marriage supper of the Lamb are portrayed as divorcees.

5. The imagery is built on a Genesis 2:24 marriage.

Some questions

1. Why do you think God might use allusions rather than always 'speak plainly'?

2. Do you think the Samaritan woman understood what Jesus was saying— if so, what specifically in the encounter with Jesus makes you think that?

3. Should this New Testament marital imagery impact our understanding of, and practical approach to, divorce and those that have been divorced?

Chapter 6: Genesis 2:24 in the New Testament

6.1   Introduction

Chapter 2 demonstrated that Genesis 2:23 and Genesis 2:24 underpin two different conceptual domains:

Genesis 2:23	Genesis 2:24
1. A miraculous man and woman.	1. A naturally born man and woman.
2. Remain as they are.	2. Choose to become what they were not.
3. In a literal one-flesh union.	3. In a metaphoric one-flesh union.
4. Without the need for a covenant.	4. By means of a covenant.

Although it is widely thought that Genesis 2:24 refers to the marriage of Adam and Eve, chapter 3 demonstrated that the legislation and narratives of the Old Testament show that subsequent marriages in ancient Israel embodied the Genesis 2:24 principles, principles that are mutually exclusive to those that formed the primal couple marriage.

Chapter 4 showed that the marriage of God to Israel was also based on Genesis 2:24 principles, and that the source domain of this imagery was the understanding of marriage in Israel.

In chapter 5 we saw that the New Testament marital imagery flowed seamlessly from that Old Testament imagery. Jesus is explicitly described as the bridegroom by John the Baptist, and his earthly ministry can be understood as an extended betrothal period inviting all humanity, Jew and Gentile, to the wedding supper of the Lamb. Jesus held out the offer of a Genesis 2:24 marriage, whereby naturally born men and women, could become what they were not, the people of God, by means of volitional covenant. None of these concepts are seen in Adam and Eve's marriage. It is clear that the marital imagery of the New Testament is firmly rooted in a Genesis 2:24 marriage.

We can now portray the situation diagrammatically:

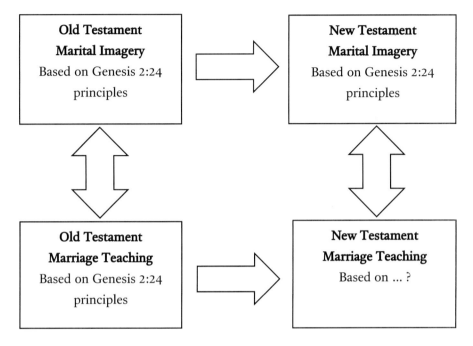

Perhaps the reader can already see the issue? Old Testament marriage teaching and practice is based on Genesis 2:24 principles. Those principles form the source domain of the Old Testament imagery, and thus human marriage and the marriage imagery are consonant. The New Testament marital imagery follows on from the Old Testament imagery and embraces the same principles—all clearly rooted in Genesis 2:24.

Any metaphoric imagery only works if the thing the reader is being asked to imagine (Jesus as a bridegroom offering a new 'marriage' to all humanity) is rooted in their experience. As Lakoff and Johnson say, 'The most fundamental values in a culture will be coherent with the metaphorical structure of the most fundamental concepts in the culture.'[31] Westbrook's comments (cited in §4.1) about the Old Testament marital imagery apply equally to the New Testament imagery:

> If God's relationship with Israel is to be explained by a metaphor
> drawing upon the everyday life of the audience then that metaphor,
> to be effective, must reflect accurately the reality known to the

audience. If the narrator were to invent the legal rules on which the metaphor is based, it would cease to be a valid metaphor.[32]

In the Bible's marital imagery, the *Divine Marriage* and human marriage 'mirror' each other—it is how conceptual metaphors work, concepts moving from one domain to the other. It follows that the New Testament marital imagery, where Jesus is portrayed as the Bridegroom Messiah, must be consonant with the understanding of marriage in New Testament times.

There is now clear documentary evidence that marriage in first century Palestine was based on Genesis 2:24 principles, not on an idealised primal couple model described in Genesis 2:23. The collection of marriage and divorce contracts discovered in Palestine dating from New Testament times show that marriage was formed by a volitional, conditional, asymmetrical covenant. These Judaean Desert Documents (referenced in §3.5) demonstrate that marriage (and divorce) practice had not changed since the time of Moses. Thus those that specialise in metaphor theory, such as Lakoff and Johnson, and the Old Testament scholar Westbrook (as cited above), have been proved correct when they said we should expect the source and target domains of a conceptual metaphor to match.

But what is even more important for our study, we might expect that the New Testament writers would *teach* a marriage based on Genesis 2:24 principles, otherwise their marriage teaching would contradict their marriage imagery. We do not have to read far to be reassured about the Bible's conceptual integrity in this matter—both Matthew and Mark record Jesus saying that the model for marriage is indeed to be found in Genesis 2:24. However, the Christian church, from post-apostolic times, has understood that when the New Testament uses Genesis 2:24 it is referring to Adam and Eve. As a consequence, it is thought that Genesis 2:24 refers to a marriage with a heavenly, or at least a mystical, dimension and many believe that such is formed by sexual intercourse. And thus the church has believed that the New Testament teaches a new model for marriage for the Christian era—a marriage model that contradicts its own marital imagery.

The task in this chapter is to try and see if that perception stands up to scrutiny. To do that, we will examine each citation of Genesis 2:24 and see if we can determine its meaning in context, and whether that meaning is different from the way it was understood by ancient Israel.

6.2   Genesis 2:24 in the New Testament

Genesis 2:24 is cited in: Matthew 19, Mark 10, 1 Corinthians 6, and Ephesians 5. In each case Genesis 2:24 is employed to make a point of considerable theological significance, they are: the understanding of marriage and divorce (the Gospels); the nature of the body of Christ (1 Corinthians 6); and the reason for the Gentile hope (Ephesians 5). To misunderstand the meaning of the verse means that there is the potential to go wrong in all these key New Testament teachings. The Gospel verses will be looked at in chapter 7, so the focus here will be on Paul's use of Genesis 2:24.

The consensus view that the New Testament writers have a different understanding of marriage and Genesis 2:24 than ancient Israel is for many an unarticulated assumption. An exception is William Loader, who makes a detailed linguistic argument to suggest that the New Testament writers, or at least Paul, deliberately gave the verse a new meaning.

Loader's argument goes like this. The Hebrew word for flesh (*basar*) when translated into Greek is *sarx* — and Paul, writing in Greek uses that *sarx* word. This, Loader claims, 'puts the emphasis more on sexual union.'[33] But the question to be asked is: Would that have been Paul's intention? It is certainly true that whenever Paul quotes Genesis 2:24 he does so from the Greek Septuagint Old Testament. Although Paul almost certainly would have known the Hebrew Bible text, the most common translation of the Old Testament available in the churches would have been the Septuagint, so many of the citations of the Old Testament in the New Testament, including Paul's, are from that version.

The aim of the Septuagint translators was to faithfully render the meaning of their sacred Hebrew text to the best of their ability. But anybody who has tried to learn a foreign language soon realises that many words in one language do not have an exact equivalence in another and compromises must be made. But if that is the case, it does not mean that the translator *intended* to change any meaning, and such would have certainly been unthinkable to the Jewish scholars who worked on the Septuagint.

Paul was both a scholar and a 'Hebrew of the Hebrews' (Philippians 3:5) so he would have known the original Hebrew meaning of the term 'one flesh' (that is, one family). We can see from Galatians 3:16 (NIV) how careful he is about the very words of the text of the Hebrew Bible:

> The promises were spoken to Abraham and to his seed. Scripture does not say "and to seeds," meaning many people, but "and to your seed," meaning one person, who is Christ.

So it is seems highly unlikely that he would have allowed his use of the Greek word *sarx* (flesh) to dramatically change the understanding of the Hebrew word *basar* (flesh, meaning family)— without even mentioning it.

In light of these arguments, we will now consider Paul's use of Genesis 2:24 in context, because if it can be shown that he understood Genesis 2:24 in the way ancient Israel did, this will inform our understanding of his teaching on marriage.

6.3   Genesis 2:24 in Ephesians 5:31–32

> "Therefore a man shall leave his father and mother and hold fast to his wife, and the two shall become one flesh." This mystery is profound, and I am saying that it refers to Christ and the church. (Ephesians 5:31–32)

These two verses, in effect, make the classic pair-wise falsely literal metaphoric A 'is' B statement—that is, GENESIS 2:24 IS CHRIST AND THE CHURCH. Thus Genesis 2:24 is specifically stated to be the source domain of the imagery contained in the target domain—the relationship of Christ and the church. Paul here clearly articulates the structure map of the New Testament marital imagery. However, as has been pointed out, the conflation of Genesis 2:23 with Genesis 2:24, in the minds of scholars, has led them to understand that the author is saying Adam and Eve refer to Christ and the church. A recent example (2014) is that of G. K. Beale and Benjamin Gladd:

> the Old Testament conception of marriage properly understood finds its roots in Genesis 2:24. The Israelites were to hearken back to Adam and Eve's marriage in the garden as the fountainhead of all Israelite marriage.... Since the primeval couple's marriage [i.e.

Adam and Eve] was the template for future marriages, we must keep
Genesis 2:24 in mind when we study the marriage metaphor
between the Lord and Israel.... Israel was to model her behaviour
after Eve and remain faithful to her Adamic husband, the Lord. With
the Old Testament context of Genesis 2:24 in mind, we will now
return to Ephesians 5:31–32.[34]

Thus the primal couple is read into Genesis 2:24 and seen to be both the
model for subsequent marriages and the basis of the Bible's marital imagery.
In Ephesians 5, because the referent of Genesis 2:24 is thought to be the
primal couple, and Romans 5:14 and 2 Corinthians 11:2–3 make it clear that
the primal couple typologically prefigure Christ and the church,
commentators pursue an exegesis based on *typology,* rather than seeing that
Paul is enunciating the root metaphor of the New Testament metaphoric
marital imagery.

Typology is when a past event prefigures a future event, one that usually has
a Christological dimension. An example is the serpent on the pole that Jesus
refers to in John 3:14, making a comparison between that event and his own
death, 'And as Moses lifted up the serpent in the wilderness, so must the Son
of Man be lifted up.' This is typology, in that the serpent on the pole was an
actual 'once only' event in the past that pointed to (or 'prefigured') an event
in the future—Christ's own death.

Thus Beale and Gladd, with their understanding that Genesis 2:24 refers to
Adam and Eve, state that, *"The revealed mystery in Ephesians 5 therefore refers
to Paul's perception that Adam and Eve's union in marriage typologically
corresponds to Christ and the church."*[35]

But Adam and Eve's marriage—a 'once only' event in the past (like the
serpent on the pole) typologically prefigures a future event, that is, the
wedding, and consequent Christ/church union, at the end of time.
Carmichael points out that at the marriage supper of the Lamb, Christ in
effect 'marries' his own body as did Adam with Eve, fulfilling, he believes,
that Edenic ideal.[36] The typology can be set out like this:

Adam and Eve	Christ and the Church at the End of Time
1. Adam, a miraculously created man.	1. Christ, a miraculously conceived man.
2. Eve, miraculously made from Adam.	2. The church, miraculously brought into being by the Holy Spirit.
3. Adam marries Eve, his own body.	3. Christ marries the church, his own body.
4. In a union formed by God.	4. In a union formed by God.

In contrast, in Ephesians 5:31–32, Paul is articulating the structure map of the New Testament metaphoric marital imagery, where we have the A 'is' B false literalism. Unlike typology, that looks to a past event to illustrate a future event, the metaphoric marital imagery portrays a contemporary and ongoing situation of a bridegroom seeking his bride. Thus this New Testament imagery cross-maps the four key features of mundane (i.e. non-miraculous) marriage, outlined in chapter 2, to the Christ/church relationship:

Genesis 2:24	Christ and the Church
1. A naturally born man and woman.	1. Naturally born men and women.
2. Choose to become what they were not.	2. Choose to become what they were not.
3. In a metaphoric one-flesh union.	3. In a metaphoric one-flesh union.
4. By means of a volitional covenant.	4. By means of a volitional covenant.

So the mystery now revealed lies not, as some believe, in human marriage itself, or in the Christ/church union, or that Adam and Eve's relationship corresponds to Christ and the church (as per Beale and Gladd). The mystery is rather in the identity of the members of the body of Christ, in that they include a people who were considered to be outside God's covenant, but who now can become what they were not, the people of God. Paul J. Sampley points out that the author is developing this theme from chapter two.[37] Verses 15–16 state:

> by abolishing the law of commandments and ordinances that he might create in himself one new man in place of the two, so making peace, and might reconcile us both to God in one body through the cross, thereby killing the hostility. (Ephesians 2: 15–16)

And Sampley suggests:

> When a substantive like [mystery] is used six times in such crucial places as it is in Ephesians, there is considerable probability of some lines of continuity of meaning between the uses in the different contexts.[38]

But Sampley, as with most scholars, does not reference any metaphoric concepts, and believes that Genesis 2:24 refers to the primal couple. In so doing he acknowledges the struggle that many exegetes, including himself, have in establishing the meaning of the reference to Genesis 2:24. Nonetheless Sampley sees, as I am suggesting, that the *mystery* of Ephesians 5:32 is the incorporation of Gentile and Jew into the one body, he comments, 'The recipients of Ephesians are urged to recognise that they, together with Jews, share in God's cosmic purposes.'[39]

Thus Ephesians 5:31–32 links the Christ/church relationship and the inclusion of the Gentiles with the human marital affinity relationship of Genesis 2:24, whereby an unrelated couple on marriage can be counted as being in one family. Galatians 3:16 (NIV) states:

> The promises were spoken to Abraham and to his seed. Scripture does not say "and to seeds," meaning many people, but "and to your seed," meaning one person, who is Christ.

It is clear Paul sees that the promise to Abraham is fulfilled in Christ. When the believing community becomes the bride of Christ they, by means of the Genesis 2:24 affinity union, become a member of Christ's family. Thus Galatians 3:29 says: 'And if you are Christ's, then you are Abraham's offspring, heirs according to promise'—that is, not by blood. This contrasts with Israel, who Paul explains in his Galatians 4:21–31 allegory, was like Hagar, 'born according to the flesh'—that is, she represents an understanding of a blood relationship with Abraham.

Israel's hope was in that blood line descent from Abraham—their boast was that they came *from* Abraham. But here in Ephesians the Gentile hope is declared to be in the conceptual domain of Genesis 2:24—just as a married couple come *into* their one-flesh union, so it is that the Gentiles can become what they were not, and come *into* a relationship with Christ, Abraham's promised seed. Such appears to be underpinned by the Hebrew text, as mentioned in §2.3, in that v. 23 uses the Hebrew preposition *Mem* to describe Eve coming *from* Adam, in contrast, v. 24 uses the *Lamed* to describe the couple coming *into* their new union—but this has been lost in most modern translations. The clash of concepts runs through the New Testament and is clearly seen in Jesus's exchange with the Pharisees as recorded in John 8.

Like a wife who, although not a blood relation of her husband, is *counted as* being a member of his family by means of the marital covenantal union (symbolised when a bride changes her family name)—so it is that the members of Christ's bridal community are *counted as* being in Abraham's family. Romans 9:8 explains it this way: 'This means that it is not the children of the flesh who are the children of God, but the children of the promise are counted as offspring.'

The argument is further strengthened when it is considered that in Romans 9:22–29 the inclusion of the Gentiles is linked to the promised 'remarriage' in the marital imagery as foretold by Hosea: 'Those who were not my people I will call "my people."' This is how the promise to Abraham's offspring is reconciled with the Old Testament promises to include the Gentiles, and is the profound mystery referenced in Ephesians 5:32—the seed of Abraham is the Bridegroom Messiah.

Thus Ephesians 5:22–33 is portraying Jew and Gentile together forming one body (with Christ as the head) and one bride (with Christ as the bridegroom) in a marriage to be consummated at the end of time when they will become one flesh with their 'husband.' Thus Paul sees a *sensus plenior* (a fuller or deeper meaning) in Genesis 2:24 foreshadowing redemptive history and the inclusion of the Gentiles. It is a breath-taking insight that Paul has been given into that Genesis 2:24 teaching, and how God's promised redemption of many different people groups in the one seed of Abraham is to be achieved.

The 'profound mystery,' God's plan of redemption, is not (and never was) based on a blood line descent from Abraham via his seed Jacob, but with the marital covenantal union that Genesis 2:24 speaks of. Anybody in union with Christ, anybody that by faith has chosen to be in his bridal community by means of the volitional covenant that he has offered, will be counted among the people of God. They include, as Hebrews 11 makes clear, all the believers of Old Testament times.

6.4   When Concepts Collide

It has been seen that metaphors take something from everyday life to illustrate something else, a new idea, a new concept. As an example, we looked at the Bible's teaching that Jesus is the good shepherd, and how that teaching creates the idea that God could be thought of as a shepherd to us. We called the everyday life illustration the source domain, and the thing it illustrated the target domain—and drew this map to help us imagine it:

MAP 2: JESUS IS THE GOOD SHEPHERD

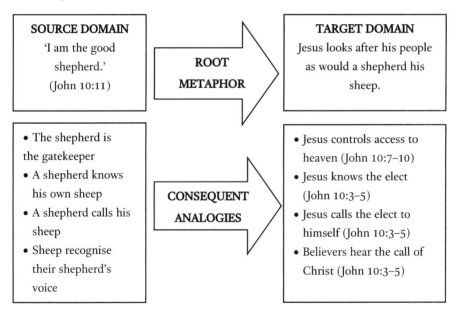

Our metaphor maps so far show that the metaphors go *from* one concept *to* another concept—a new concept, a new understanding, that is created by the metaphor. They all have had an 'earthly' concept that is used to illustrate a 'spiritual' concept—so we have: THE LORD IS MY SHEPHERD; GOD IS THE HUSBAND OF ISRAEL; JESUS IS BRIDEGROOM OF THE CHURCH. Thus shepherds, husbands, and bridegrooms, are all used to tell us something about God and his relationship with his people.

But there is another sort of metaphor that takes two things, or concepts, that already exist, and pushes them together, and the resulting 'collision' creates a new idea. An example of this is how we understand Jesus Christ. We know that Jesus is the Messiah (Messiah means the 'anointed one') that the Old Testament had long foretold would come. But the Old Testament concept of a Messiah was very different from the baby that arrived at Bethlehem. The Old Testament Messiah was to be a great warrior king, in contrast, Jesus was a supposed illegitimate child of lowly birth who worked as a carpenter and spoke in his ministry of peace and love. Nonetheless, it became clear to the early believers that Jesus really is the Messiah the Old Testament spoke of. And so they came to call him Jesus the 'anointed one,' or Jesus the Christ (from *Christos*, the Greek for anointed)—or simply, Jesus Christ.

So two concepts, a victorious king of Israel, and a crucified son of a carpenter become, in our minds, one person, Jesus Christ. This is not source to target mapping, but what we might call merged mapping, where two things are welded, or 'mashed' together in our minds.

Diagrammatically, such merged mapping to create a new, third idea, might be imagined like this:

Jesus (the) Christ

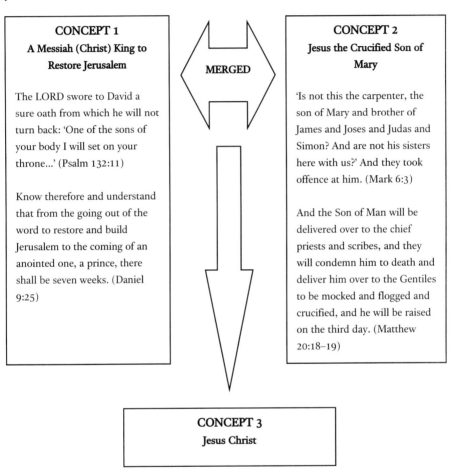

CONCEPT 1
A Messiah (Christ) King to Restore Jerusalem

The LORD swore to David a sure oath from which he will not turn back: 'One of the sons of your body I will set on your throne...' (Psalm 132:11)

Know therefore and understand that from the going out of the word to restore and build Jerusalem to the coming of an anointed one, a prince, there shall be seven weeks. (Daniel 9:25)

MERGED

CONCEPT 2
Jesus the Crucified Son of Mary

'Is not this the carpenter, the son of Mary and brother of James and Joses and Judas and Simon? And are not his sisters here with us?' And they took offence at him. (Mark 6:3)

And the Son of Man will be delivered over to the chief priests and scribes, and they will condemn him to death and deliver him over to the Gentiles to be mocked and flogged and crucified, and he will be raised on the third day. (Matthew 20:18–19)

CONCEPT 3
Jesus Christ

This might be imagined as baking a cake, when flour and eggs are whisked together, placed in the oven, and out comes a cake! Although we know flour and eggs are in the cake, we don't see them as separate things—we see (and taste) one new thing—the cake. So it is with our concept of Jesus Christ, we have merged two ideas—a victorious King, and a baby born in the manger—but we just think of one person, the Lord Jesus Christ.

6.5   Genesis 2:24 in 1 Corinthians 6: The Body of Christ

The Bible considers all believers to be one Christian *family*—Paul frequently calling fellow believers brothers, or sisters (e.g. Romans 1:13). Another description of us in the Bible is *the body of Christ*. They are two very closely related concepts. But where do these ideas come from?

In 2 Samuel 5:1 it can be seen that Israel considered themselves to be united in a 'one-flesh' union: 'Then all the tribes of Israel came to David at Hebron and said, "Behold, we are your bone and flesh."' Israel believed that they were in a 'vertical' metaphoric marital relationship with God, but it is clear they also perceived themselves to be in a 'horizontal' one-flesh/one family relationship with each other—as indeed they were, in that they were all great, great ... grandchildren of Jacob. They were one big family.

Paul tells us in 1 Corinthians 6 how he formed the idea that, just like Israel, all Christians also form one family. We have seen that when a man and a woman marry in a Genesis 2:24 union they do not just become a couple, they become 'one flesh,' that is, they create a new family unit. In this passage in 1 Corinthians 6 Paul brings the Genesis 2:24 one-flesh (i.e. one family) concept together with all the believers at Corinth, and says that all the believers at Corinth are in a one-flesh union—that is, one family:

> Do you not know that your bodies are members of Christ? ... For, as it is written, "The two will become one flesh." (1 Corinthians 6:15–16)

He takes the 'one-flesh/one family' identity from Genesis 2:24, and merges it with all believers. In other words, he takes the kinship identity that Israel had by means of their blood line descent from Jacob, and applies that understanding to Christian believers, who collectively have a marital covenantal union with Christ: all now are perceived to be 'brothers' and 'sisters' in Christ, a new family group—in effect, a new Israel. The two concepts, the one family union of Genesis 2:24, and Christian believers, having been merged, give rise to the idea in our minds that the church is one large family.

It is a small step then from the idea that the church is a family, to the concept that each family member has a different role. Paul takes that step, and elsewhere in this, and in his other letters, he develops the 'one family' idea so that we can see that the church is a functioning 'body' — a body that takes the place of Christ's physical presence on earth — the *body of Christ*.

These concepts might be illustrated like this:

MAP 6 The one family body of Christ

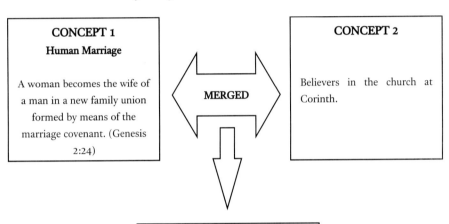

The *body of Christ* idea is rather like our cake, in that you do not think of the ingredients, of how it was made, you just see the cake, or in this case, that all Christians are in one big family — and all form part of one functioning 'body.'

6.6   Genesis 2:24 in 1 Corinthians 6: The Body of a Prostitute

In the same passage, Paul talks of a prostitute, and many Christians think that Paul is referring to literal prostitutes, and that sexual intercourse with such creates a 'one flesh' marital union.

> Do you not know that your bodies are members of Christ? Shall I then take the members of Christ and make them members of a prostitute? Never! Or do you not know that he who is joined to a prostitute becomes one body with her? For, as it is written, "The two will become one flesh." (1 Corinthians 6:15–16)

But *is* that what Paul is saying? If we look at these verses carefully, he is once more merging two concepts. One of the concepts is the same—Genesis 2:24, but this time he merges it not with the *believers* at Corinth, but with people in the church who are behaving as if they were *unbelievers*. The result is a different 'cake'—this time he calls it not the *body of Christ*, but the *body of a prostitute*. This group of people is the precise *opposite* of the church. Although at first sight this perhaps looks an improbable analysis, the same concept can be seen in Revelation 17, where the unbelieving world is described as a prostitute. Lyn Huber says of that imagery in Revelation:

> the images of harlot and bride depict two possible forms of existence for the Christian community. The community can live in idolatry, as a prostitute, or the community can live in faithfulness to God, as a bride. [40]

Paul, having spoken in the previous chapter of the sexual immorality of at least one of the church members in Corinth, says:

> Or do you not know that the unrighteous will not inherit the kingdom of God? Do not be deceived: neither the sexually immoral, nor idolaters, nor adulterers, nor men who practice homosexuality, nor thieves, nor the greedy, nor drunkards, nor revilers, nor swindlers will inherit the kingdom of God. And such were some of you. But you were washed, you were sanctified, you were justified in the name of the Lord Jesus Christ and by the Spirit of our God. (1 Corinthians 6:9–11)

It is in this context, seemingly in exasperation, that Paul accuses some Corinthians (vv. 15–16), of becoming 'one flesh' with a prostitute. He knew the Old Testament thoroughly, having studied with Gamaliel, a leading scholar of his day (Acts 22:3). He knew that when Israel behaved like the unbelieving nations around them, the prophets usually accused them of 'prostitution.' Indeed, Ezekiel declares of Israel (or rather Judah as it was then): 'Therefore, O prostitute, hear the word of the LORD' (Ezekiel 16:35). He is speaking to Judah (God's 'wife') about her idolatry. This is what had caused their Babylonian exile, and Ezekiel portrays this behaviour as Judah prostituting herself. In other words, the prophet is saying (consonant with all the Old Testament imagery) that Judah collectively, *is* the prostitute—and individual members of the tribe are, in effect, considered by him to be members of that prostitute. Ezekiel is not saying that all the members of the tribe of Judah were visiting prostitutes.

It seems Paul is using that same imagery here in 1 Corinthians 6, when he suggests that some members of the church at Corinth are going back to their old life and behaving not like Christian believers, but like a prostitute. In this imagery, these church members are, like Judah, not visiting prostitutes, they *are* the prostitute, and the individuals are members of her.

To paraphrase him, he says:

> You Corinthian Christians used to belong to the unbelieving community, but now that you belong to the believing church community, you are joined to Christ in a Genesis 2:24 one family (one-flesh) union—you are collectively one family, the body of Christ. So do not go back to that unbelieving community and become a family member there, do not become one family (one-flesh) with a "prostitute"! Instead be one body (one family) with Christ.

So this time Paul merges Genesis 2:24 with unbelievers, generating the idea that unbelievers are also in one family, in one 'body.' If we go back to our cake analogy, Paul has mixed together the one family Genesis 2:24 union with the unbelieving world and produced a new concept—*the body of a prostitute*—the precise opposite of *the body of Christ*.

If we were to draw a map it might look like this:

MAP 7 The one family 'Body of a Prostitute'

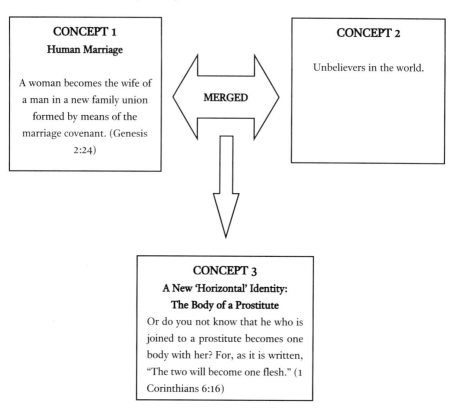

The Christian consensus literal prostitute interpretation has impacted our understanding of marriage. Many believe that 1 Corinthians 6 teaches that a marriage is made when sexual intercourse occurs, and such is the essence of marriage. It follows that without sexual intercourse there is no marriage— and that sexual intercourse with anybody *not* your spouse automatically terminates the marriage, or at least gives grounds for divorce.

The logic is that because sexual intercourse with somebody has created a reality in heaven, the only way this can be undone, or give grounds to be undone, is by having sexual intercourse with somebody else. Thus, for many church groupings today, illicit sexual intercourse is required to be demonstrated to dissolve a marriage—just as it used to be in UK law.

The marriage covenant is clearly linked with our sexuality, sexual intercourse being a marital expectation. But in biblical understanding, it does not *make* the marriage. The difference between marriage and the marriage act can perhaps be illustrated by considering the difference between a driving licence and driving a car: the licence permits you to drive a car, but driving a car does not give you a licence. Just as in biblical understanding marriage means sexual intercourse is permitted, but sexual intercourse does not make you married.

One argument against the analysis above, where I suggest that Paul used the term 'prostitute' to portray an unbelieving community, is that the believers at Corinth would not have understood it that way. Although the prostitute imagery is used extensively in the Old Testament the Corinthian church was predominantly a Gentile church—so how could they possibly know about that?

But as has already been seen (§1.5), in 1 Corinthians 5 there are some subtle and quite complex allusions to Old Testament concepts that Paul either believes that whoever delivered the letter (perhaps Timothy) was going to explain, or he assumes the readers of the letter had sufficient knowledge of the Old Testament to understand his argument. It is also possible that Paul, in the time he had spent with the Corinthians before he wrote the letter, had spoken of the Old Testament marital imagery, where ungodly behaviour by Israel is nearly always described as prostitution.

But perhaps the strongest argument for the analysis I have given, is that Paul employs Genesis 2:24 to form both the idea of the body of Christ, *and* the body of a prostitute. No exegete would suggest that when Paul links Genesis 2:24 to the body of Christ that he is thinking of sexual intercourse—so why apply that understanding to his second use of the same verse? In other words, it is difficult to see how the verse can be used to represent one thing (a covenantal one family agreement), in one half of the illustration, and another thing (sexual intercourse), in the other half of the *same* illustration— and it be assumed that the reader would understand the illustration that way.

For all these reasons, it seems clear in 1 Corinthians 6:15–16 that Paul is saying you become a member of a prostitute's 'body' in the same way you become a member of Christ's 'body'—by means of a one family, covenantal agreement, not a sexual act—the one family, covenantal agreement, being the understanding of the Genesis 2:24 union in ancient Israel.

There are other exegetes who, like me, understand that Paul was speaking of the believing and unbelieving communities in 1 Corinthians 6:15–16, and not a literal sex worker. Even so, it is true to say that only a minority holds this view. Yet when the passage is analysed in light of the broader perspective of the Bible's metaphoric marital imagery, which runs from the beginning of Genesis to the end of the book of Revelation, it seems clear that Paul is writing in that same tradition. And in so doing, he uses Genesis 2:24 with its historical biblical meaning of a volitional covenant creating a new family unit.

6.7   Summary

From our analysis it seems clear that Paul does not give Genesis 2:24 a new meaning for the church age—he does not see it as a reference to either Adam and Eve or sexual intercourse. In every citation he understands, just as ancient Israel did, that it speaks of a covenantal one family affinity union. Thus it seems reasonable to expect, that when the verse is cited by Jesus in his marriage and divorce teaching, it should be understood in that same way. It is to that teaching we now turn.

Some key points

1. The word 'flesh' in Genesis 2:24, when translated into Greek and used in the New Testament, retains its Old Testament 'family' meaning.

2. In Ephesians 5:31–32 Paul uses Genesis 2:24 to show how the Gentiles can be counted as being Abraham's seed and thus be included in the promise God made to him.

3. In 1 Corinthians 6:15–16 Paul uses Genesis 2:24 to describe how believers are members of the body of Christ, and have a 'one family' relationship with each other, just as the people of Israel had.

4. In 1 Corinthians 6:15–16 Paul uses Genesis 2:24 to show how some in the church at Corinth were behaving as if they members of a 'prostitute,' that is, part of the unbelieving world. In doing this he was standing in the tradition of Old Testament prophetic marital imagery, for example, Ezekiel 16:35 — a tradition that John in Revelation followed.

Some questions

1. How likely do you think it is that Paul intended to change the meaning of Genesis 2:24 when he quoted it?

2. Do you think that the Corinthians would have understood the prostitute imagery?

3. If so, why? If not, why not?

Chapter 7: Divorce and Remarriage in the Gospels

7.1   Introduction

The apparent consensus among New Testament scholars and the church is that the one-flesh marriage of the primal couple is introduced (or restored) in New Testament teaching as the model for human marriage. Based on this, various church groupings have adopted teaching that, in summary, forbids: divorce (the Church of Rome);[41] remarriage after divorce while the divorced partner lives (the Church of England);[42] remarriage after divorce for the 'innocent party,' and remarriage after desertion if the deserting partner is not a believer (many independent churches).[43] However, these various divorce and remarriage restrictions are not reflected in the legislation or marital practices of the Old Testament, or in its marital imagery (chapters 3 & 4).

Chapter 5 demonstrated that the source and target domains of New Testament imagery were congruent, both being based on the Old Testament understanding of the volitional, conditional, covenantal marital union of Genesis 2:24. It might be argued that this does not negate the possibility that the New Testament writers adopted a primal couple model as the basis for their marriage teaching, but this would mean that they were repudiating in their teaching the marriage model they employed in their imagery: a model of marriage familiar to contemporary society—one that the Bridegroom Messiah is portrayed in the Gospels as fulfilling in some detail, and which climaxes in the Apocalypse when he is seen to take the elect, including it seems the elect of 'divorced' Israel, into a new 'marriage.'

Furthermore, we need to consider whether, in speaking of his own divorce and remarriage, God would portray himself as doing something that was against his own law. Although it must be accepted that the marital imagery sometimes portrays things that would not happen in normal marriages—for example, where the bride is a building coming down from heaven at the end of Revelation; or when God is portrayed as being married to two 'sisters' (the divided nation, Israel and Judah) when such is forbidden in Leviticus 18:18— however, God married only the one 'woman,' Israel, the division of the nation occurring later. Nonetheless, as the central theme of all the Bible's marital imagery from Genesis to Revelation is God's divorce and remarriage of his people, it is unthinkable that divorce and remarriage would be forbidden in God's law for human marriage. It would mean that God was treating his own marriage differently to human marriage, and thus defeating the whole point of the imagery, which is to illustrate his relationship with his people from the human marriage perspective.

For all these reasons, it is suggested that it should be possible to find an exegesis of New Testament divorce and remarriage teaching that is consonant with its own marital imagery, and that is the aim of this chapter.

Chapter 6 looked at the use of Genesis 2:24 by Paul. We now turn to the two key Gospel passages that reference Genesis 2:24 in their divorce and remarriage teaching, set out below in chart form.[44]

Matthew 19:3–9 and Mark 10:2–12

Matthew 19	Mark 10
Pharisees' Question	*Pharisees' Question*
And Pharisees came up to him and tested him by asking, "Is it lawful to divorce one's wife for any cause?" (19:3)	And Pharisees came up and in order to test him asked, "Is it lawful for a man to divorce his wife?" (10:2)
From the Beginning	*Moses's Teaching*
He answered, "Have you not read that he who created them from the beginning made them male and female, and said, 'Therefore a man shall leave his father and his mother and hold fast to his wife, and the two shall become one flesh'? So they are no longer two but one flesh. What therefore God has joined together, let not man separate." (19:4–6)	He answered them, "What did Moses command you?" They said, "Moses allowed a man to write a certificate of divorce and to send her away." And Jesus said to them, "Because of your hardness of heart he wrote you this commandment." (10:3–5)

Moses's Teaching	From the Beginning
They said to him, "Why then did Moses command one to give a certificate of divorce and to send her away?" He said to them, "Because of your hardness of heart Moses allowed you to divorce your wives, but from the beginning it was not so." (19:7–8)	"But from the beginning of creation, 'God made them male and female.' 'Therefore a man shall leave his father and mother and hold fast to his wife, and the two shall become one flesh.' So they are no longer two but one flesh. What therefore God has joined together, let not man separate." (10:6–9)
Answering the Question	
"And I say to you: whoever divorces his wife, except for sexual immorality, and marries another, commits adultery." (19:9)	*Answering the Question*
	And in the house the disciples asked him again about this matter. And he said to them, "Whoever divorces his wife and marries another commits adultery against her, and if she divorces her husband and marries another, she commits adultery." (10:10–12)

7.2   The Pharisees' Question

Most scholars now see that 'any cause' in Matthew 19:3 is a reference to a contemporary debate about the meaning of the 'some indecency' teaching in Deuteronomy 24:1–4 that we have already referred to (§3.5).

> When a man takes a wife and marries her, if then she finds no favour in his eyes because he has found some indecency in her, and he writes her a certificate of divorce and puts it in her hand and sends her out of his house, and she departs out of his house, and if she goes and becomes another man's wife, and the latter man hates her and writes her a certificate of divorce and puts it in her hand and sends her out of his house, or if the latter man dies, who took her to be his wife, then her former husband, who sent her away, may not take her again to be his wife, after she has been defiled, for that is an

abomination before the LORD. And you shall not bring sin upon the land that the LORD your God is giving you for an inheritance. (Deuteronomy 24:1–4)

One group of Pharisees thought that the Hebrew text meant that the divorce was for any cause *of* indecency, but another group thought that the teaching meant that divorce was for any cause *and* indecency. Not surprisingly it became known as the *any cause* debate. The question was, 'What was it that Moses was allowing divorce for?' The subtext was, 'Would Jesus give a direct answer to such a contentious question?' We can see from the Gospel account that Jesus *did* give a direct answer. He explained that Moses was teaching that a husband can only divorce his wife for any 'sexual immorality' by her.

7.3   From the Beginning

God Made Them Male and Female

In Matthew 19:4 (and similarly Mark 10:6) Jesus says, 'Have you not read that he who created them from the beginning made them male and female.' This is clearly a reference to Genesis 1:27 and Adam and Eve. Jesus is saying that this is how creation started out, people were to be one of two complementary genders designed to be able to come together in a sexual union.

But rather than saying, as some believe, that the way Adam and Eve were made, or the way they were brought together, is the *pattern* for subsequent marriages, Jesus is recorded as quoting Genesis 2:24. And as we have seen, it is this Genesis 2:24 marriage, not Adam and Eve's marriage, that is the pattern for all subsequent Old Testament marriages, and those marriages have many features that clearly differentiate them from the marriage of Adam and Eve. Adam and Eve were formed during the initial acts of creation, from which God 'rested' (Gen 2:2–3), and subsequently, as in the rest of creation, a different set of principles operate as the world turns and seasons come and go.

What God has Joined Together, Let Not Man Separate

But this reference to Adam and Eve, and the conflation of Genesis 2:23 with Genesis 2:24, has caused many to believe that in this conversation, Adam and

Eve's marriage is being affirmed, or reaffirmed, as the ongoing model for marriage for human kind. And thus when Jesus says, 'What God has joined together let not man separate,' it is thought that, just as in Adam and Eve's marriage, God puts every *subsequent* marriage together, and therefore there can be no divorce. In other words, it is believed that God is directly involved in forming each marriage and thus it has a heavenly dimension—a 'marriage made in heaven.'

However, it is highly unlikely that the Pharisees would have understood Jesus this way—it would have been such a radical departure from any contemporary Jewish understanding that it would have needed a whole separate discourse to explain. As has been seen (§3.2), ancient Israel was a theocracy and there were many tabernacle/temple ceremonies controlled by the priesthood that dominated national life—but marriage was not one of them.

Marriage (and divorce) was a private matter between the couple themselves and their respective families, and was not mediated by any priest or elder—there is no record of any religious or state involvement of any sort. So while it was understood that God's plan for his creation included marriage, the absence of any religious ceremony indicates that there was not a concept that God formed *each* marriage. Notwithstanding a high view of providence that many evangelicals rightly hold, the view that God specifically puts together every marriage (however defined) gives rise to many ethical and theological difficulties.

What is more, it seems clear that Matthew would not have understood Jesus in the way that some Christians understand him, that is, teaching that marriage has a heavenly dimension—because in chapter 22 he reports this encounter between Jesus and the Sadducees:

> The same day Sadducees came to him, who say that there is no resurrection, and they asked him a question, saying, "Teacher, Moses said, 'If a man dies having no children, his brother must marry the widow and raise up children for his brother.' Now there were seven brothers among us. The first married and died, and having no children left his wife to his brother. So too the second and third, down to the seventh. After them all, the woman died. In the

> resurrection, therefore, of the seven, whose wife will she be? For they
> all had her." But Jesus answered them, "You are wrong, because you
> know neither the Scriptures nor the power of God. For in the
> resurrection they neither marry nor are given in marriage, but are
> like angels in heaven." (Matthew 22:23–30)

In other words, there is no heavenly aspect to marriage (excepting that it
illustrates the relationship between Christ and the church). Thus it is far more
likely that when Jesus says, 'what God has joined together,' he is referring to
marriage as a creation institution—not that God puts every individual
marriage together, as Craig Blomberg points out.[45] And when God gave
marriage he also gave with it teaching that applies to all mankind—thus
Jesus's comment 'let not man separate' would indicate that mankind should
not make up their own rules for marriage and divorce (*contra* the position of
many today). In summary, before tackling their question about divorce, Jesus
was taking the Pharisees back to first principles.

7.4   Moses's Teaching

The Certificate of Divorce

Undeterred by this comment of Jesus emphasising the principles of marriage,
the Pharisees go back to their question about Deuteronomy 24, 'Why then
did Moses command one to give a certificate of divorce and to send her
away?' Jesus explains that this was allowed because of the hardness of men's
hearts. Nonetheless, Jesus does not rescind this teaching. We should not be
surprised by that, as the Bible tells us that it was Moses himself who wrote
the first five books of the Bible (e.g. 2 Chronicles 25:4), under the inspiration
of God. So it is clear that God himself saw no contradiction between the
Genesis 2:24 pattern for marriage, as reaffirmed by Jesus, and the
Deuteronomy 24:1–4 teaching that allowed divorce.

This is in accord with Matthew 5:31–32:

> It was also said, "Whoever divorces his wife, let him give her a
> certificate of divorce." But I say to you that everyone who divorces
> his wife, except on the ground of sexual immorality, makes her

commit adultery. And whoever marries a divorced woman commits adultery. (Matthew 5:31–32)

The teaching of Matthew 5:27–48 is in the form of an antithesis: 'You have heard that it was said…. But I say to you.' The first part of the antithesis is the self-righteous keeping of the letter of the law typified by the scribes and Pharisees, while the second points to the true meaning of the law, a heart righteousness. If we look carefully at Matthew 5:31–32 we can see that the 'heart righteousness' in v. 32 is not a cancellation of the Mosaic law, but a clarification of it. The heart righteousness Jesus proclaimed, as we shall see below, is the Old Testament teaching — divorce for indecency *only*. In other words, he repudiates the 'divorce for indecency *and* any cause' argument.

Hard Hearts

But some believe that the teaching of Moses about divorce does not apply to Christians, as regenerate believers do not have hard hearts. But John tells us that, 'If we say we have no sin, we deceive ourselves, and the truth is not in us' (1 John 1:8). Unfortunately, even Christians can at times have hard hearts. And Douglas Moo comments:

> Both the Matthean pericopae give teaching on divorce closely similar to the Mosaic provisions. This being the case, the "hardness of heart" to which Jesus attributes the Mosaic teaching is not done away with in the new age of the Kingdom; indeed, the case of "serious sexual sin" [Greek: *porneia*] which justifies divorce is a prominent example of just that.[46]

In any case, Jesus in his conversation with the Pharisees was not talking about the concept of 'Christian' marriage, or even the marriages of Christians — he was answering the question put to him by contemporary Jewish groups about the understanding of divorce in the Hebrew Bible. Furthermore, with an understanding that Moses's 'hard hearts' concession does not apply to Christians, it is being suggested that the biblical rules (not just expectations) for the creation ordinance of marriage are different for unbelievers. Nowhere else does the Bible support such a view — God's moral laws apply to all, as Romans 1 makes clear.

7.5 Answering the Question

Matthew 5:32 has, 'except on the grounds of sexual immorality,' and Matthew 19:9, 'except for sexual immorality.' The word used for 'sexual immorality' by Matthew in both cases is the Greek word *porneia*, from which we get 'pornography.' Thus Matthew uses the word *porneia* to translate what Jesus said (if indeed Jesus did speak Aramaic rather than Greek, see §1.6), and so confirms that the Deuteronomy 24 passage *is* about sexual indecency. But even *porneia* has a certain ambiguity about it—although it seems clear that in Jesus's time *porneia* would include adultery, homosexual acts, indecent exposure, and incest.

A potential problem for those of us that see the Bible would not contradict itself, is that neither Mark 10:11 nor Luke 16:18 give this exception clause about indecency—it is only found in Matthew, in chapters 5 and 19. But as was seen in §1.1, not everything has to be said in every conversation, especially if it is a commonly held understanding.

For example, if a UK resident was asked by a visiting motorist from France what the motorway speed limit was, they would probably say 70 mph, even though there are a several exceptions to this, for example if there were road works, or a section of 'smart' motorway. But he would believe that the French motorist, an experienced driver, would understand that. And that seems to be the case here—the exception clause Matthew mentions was so obvious it did not need mentioning by every Gospel writer—divorce for sexual immorality was the universally accepted norm, both in first century Palestine, and throughout the ancient world. Nonetheless, God made sure, to avoid any doubt, that it *was* mentioned in Matthew's Gospel.

However, some confusion has been caused because *porneia* can refer to incest, and some suggest that Jesus was teaching in Matthew 19 that a marriage could only be terminated if the relationship was found to be incestuous.[47] This seems such an unlikely scenario that it would be unusual to need specific teaching by Jesus—no Pharisee or contemporary Jew would see such a marriage as valid. Surely correctly, in the divorce passages in the Gospels, most Bible versions translate *porneia* as 'sexual immorality,' or similar.

But most Bible translations opt for 'sexual immorality' when translating *porneia* in Acts 15, when Paul meets with the apostles and elders at Jerusalem to clarify what aspects of Jewish laws applied to the Gentiles. The Pentateuch gives an extensive list of marriage relationships that are forbidden and several were unique to Jewish culture (although many from Leviticus 16 and 18 form part of UK law today). Most probably the instruction to avoid *porneia* in this context means to avoid contravening those Pentateuchal incest laws.

Jesus's comment in Matthew 19:9, 'And I say to you: whoever divorces his wife, except for sexual immorality, and marries another, commits adultery'—means that a divorce initiated by the husband that was *not* based on sexual immorality is not permitted. However, Jesus does not say such a divorce could not happen, so we might say such a divorce is not a *valid* divorce. Instone-Brewer sees this as being the academic consensus and gives this analysis of the Gospel divorce teaching:

> 1. A man who marries an invalidly divorced woman commits adultery (Luke 16:18; Matthew 5:32).
>
> 2. A man who invalidly divorces his wife causes her to commit adultery (Matthew 5:32; variants of Matthew 19:9).
>
> 3. A man who invalidly divorces his wife and marries another commits adultery (Mark 10:11; Matthew 19:9; Luke 16:18).
>
> 4. A woman who invalidly divorces her husband and marries another commits adultery (Mark 10:12).[48]

What is less clear (both textually and logically) is when the 'adultery' occurs—it will be argued in §7.7 below that it is on the occasion of an invalid divorce, not on a remarriage after an invalid divorce.

7.6   Remarriage Only for the 'Innocent' Party?

It will be noticed in the above analysis, that there is no concept of seeking to identify a 'guilty' or 'innocent' party in any of the Gospel verses. When determining eligibility for remarriage the only criterion in the Gospel teaching is whether the divorce is valid. If it is, the divorce is a divorce and remarriage is valid for both parties.

Indeed, the point of getting a divorce in biblical times was to remarry—it was the reason for the certificate mentioned in Deuteronomy 24. Although a widely-held view in the Christian community is that only the 'innocent' person in any divorce can remarry, there is no teaching to that effect anywhere in Scripture, and it was certainly not the understanding in biblical times. John Murray makes this comment:

> it is difficult to discover any biblical ground on the basis of which to conclude that the remarriage of the guilty divorcee is to be considered in itself an act of adultery and as constituting an adulterous relation.[49]

This teaching was developed at the time of the Reformation. Although no uniform position was taken by the Reformers on divorce, by looking at the text of Scripture afresh, many accepted that Jesus taught that divorce was allowed, but only for 'adultery,' which they saw embraced sexual unfaithfulness by either partner. They understood that an adulterer would be put to death under Old Testament legislation (e.g. Leviticus 20:10), leaving the surviving 'innocent' marriage partner free to remarry—so they applied the logic of that situation to divorce in the church age, when unlike in ancient Israel, there would not necessarily be a mandate for the death penalty.

Although this argument had some merit, it was not based on what Jesus actually said, which was divorce for sexual immorality (however, that would include adultery). And furthermore, Jesus makes it clear that the restriction only applied to the husband. The wife's grounds for divorce, we can now see, were based, not on Deuteronomy 24, but on the more broadly based grounds articulated in Exodus 21:10–11—a teaching that Paul applies in 1 Corinthians 7 (see chapter 8). A further complication of the Reformation teaching is that there is no evidence anywhere in Scripture of the death penalty being enacted for adultery (and it certainly did not apply to David and Bathsheba, see §9.13).

So the Reformation teaching, although well intended, was based on a misunderstanding. It is flawed both theologically, and logically. Theologically, because as Murray points out (as above), there is no biblical teaching to support it. And logically, because the 'guilty' partner after a divorce is certainly divorced—so why forbid remarriage? As Christians, we have all behaved at some stage contrary to our Christian profession. And we know that Peter was forgiven for denying the Lord three times. So why is a divorcee never to be forgiven? It appears that this teaching to forbid remarriage to a divorcee is an echo of the Church of Rome's teaching that marriage is a sacrament—something happens in heaven on marriage. So they, true to their own theology, have traditionally forbidden *any* remarriage, whether a divorcee is 'guilty' or 'innocent.'

7.7   Is Remarriage Adultery?

However, if a husband divorces his wife for any reason other than sexual immorality, and goes on to marry somebody else, Jesus seems to say that in the new marriage the couple are committing adultery—such being a very specific form of sexual immorality. But we need to ask: Does Jesus mean us to take the word 'adultery' literally? I suggest in his Gospel divorce teaching that it is more likely Jesus is speaking *metaphorically*—that is, Jesus is using the term 'adultery' in the way it is used in the Bible's marital imagery. He used the expression 'adulterous generation' when referring to the Jewish people in Mark 8:

> For whoever is ashamed of me and of my words in this adulterous and sinful generation, of him will the Son of Man also be ashamed when he comes in the glory of his Father with the holy angels. (Mark 8:38)

In this comment, Jesus certainly does not mean that Jewish people were literally committing adultery, that is, that wives were being unfaithful to their husbands. Rather, he was accusing the Jewish people, as a people, of not being true to their God—by their behaviour they were breaking the covenant they had with him. This is something that the Old Testament prophets constantly accused Israel of doing, of committing 'adultery.' That is, breaking the covenant they had agreed with God at Sinai. If we apply this metaphoric understanding of adultery to the divorce teaching about human marriage in the Gospels, Jesus is saying that an invalid divorce is 'adultery'— that is, it is a break of the covenant that formed the original marriage. The 'adultery,' the breach of the covenant, is in the *divorce*, not in the *remarriage*.

Such an understanding is underpinned by the fact that adultery had a very specific definition in biblical times—that of a married woman having sexual intercourse with a man who is not her husband. It is so defined in the Law, the Prophets, and the New Testament (Leviticus 20:10; Jeremiah 29:23; Romans 7:3). It is an understanding demonstrated in the Old Testament narratives, and in the wider Ancient Near East. So when in Matthew 19:9 Jesus says, 'And I say to you: whoever divorces his wife, except for sexual immorality, and marries another, commits adultery,' his teaching, if taken literally, would not make sense to his contemporary New Testament audience, and certainly not to the Pharisees who he was addressing. A Jewish man could take another wife *without* divorcing his first wife, providing his new wife is never-married, divorced, or widowed. So it is difficult to see how a new marriage after a divorce would make him adulterous.

In other words, there is a fundamental misconception in the teaching. The same problem is in Matthew 5:32, Luke 16:18, and Mark 10:11. It might be argued that monogamy is the Christian teaching, and this certainly became the perspective of the church as they absorbed New Testament concepts. But I do not believe we can read that understanding retrospectively in to this conversation with the Pharisees about the meaning of Deuteronomy 24, and believe that they would understand Jesus's teaching that way. But they certainly would have understood the metaphoric use of 'adultery' (just as they understood Jesus when he called them 'whitewashed tombs' in Matthew 23:27)—in the Old Testament adultery is used in its metaphoric sense as much as it is in its literal sense.

It might be asked if there is no adultery in a remarriage after an invalid divorce, why remarriage was mentioned at all by Jesus in his teaching. But in biblical times it appears that divorce and remarriage were more closely linked than today—people divorced *in order to* remarry, especially a woman, as a single life for a divorced woman would be much more difficult than might be the case in the West today. If we look at Luke 16:18, based on the principles of Gospel harmonisation above (§7.5), it references two potential invalid divorces:

> Everyone who [invalidly] divorces his wife and marries another commits adultery, and he who marries a woman [invalidly] divorced from her husband commits adultery.

We might paraphrase it like this:

> Anyone who invalidly divorces his wife because he wants to marry another commits adultery, and he who marries a woman who has secured a divorce from her husband because she wants to marry her new suitor is complicit in adultery.

I suggest that this is a context sensitive paraphrase, and clarifies the fact that the focus is on the invalid divorce—the desire to marry another is what led to the 'adultery'—that is, the invalid divorce. The divorce verses in Matthew and Mark can be understood in a similar way. Although it was the case that a Jewish man did not, by law, have to divorce his first wife in order to take a second, in reality few men would have been able to support two wives. Thus in practice, a divorce would be a necessary prerequisite to any second marriage.

This argument for a metaphoric understanding of 'adultery' on an invalid divorce, not a remarriage, in the Gospels, is strengthened when it is considered that there are different manuscript versions of all the New Testament passages that teach it—a variation sometimes reflected in our modern English translations. Could it be that the early copyists took the word 'adultery' literally in these divorce passages, and thought that it applied to the remarriage, and thus had difficulty making sense of the teaching?[50]

So for all these reasons, I suggest that Jesus is saying that if a divorce is invalid it is a wrongful break of the marriage covenant—it is, as in Mark 8:38, metaphoric adultery. There is no 'adultery' (literal or metaphoric) in the new marriage. Blomberg states:

> The whole debate about whether a second marriage, following a Scripturally illegitimate divorce, is permanently adulterous or involves only an initial act of adultery dissolves. Neither is true; *the adultery (faithlessness) occurred at the time of divorce.*[51]

In chapter 9 we will look at some pastoral consequences of Jesus's teaching.

7.8   Matthew 19:10–12

> The disciples said to him, "If such is the case of a man with his wife, it is better not to marry." But he said to them, "Not everyone can receive this saying, but only those to whom it is given. For there are eunuchs who have been so from birth, and there are eunuchs who have been made eunuchs by men, and there are eunuchs who have made themselves eunuchs for the sake of the kingdom of heaven. Let the one who is able to receive this receive it."

It seems from Mark 10:10 that the disciples asked this question of Jesus later, and there is a debate about the meaning of Jesus's statement, 'Not everyone can receive this saying.' But Jesus is referring to the comment by the disciples that perhaps it is better not to marry—he was not referring to his earlier divorce teaching. Jesus is teaching that it is acceptable not to marry, this contrasted with contemporary Judaism where singleness was not valued. Paul makes a similar comment about the value of the celibate life in 1 Corinthians 7:7–8.

7.9   Mark 10:12

Mark 10:12 states:

> and if she divorces her husband and marries another, she commits adultery.

It is thought by many who hold to the traditional views about divorce that readers of Mark's Gospel would have realised that the teaching about the exception clause was in Matthew's Gospel, and would have assumed that the same applied to women. In other words, they could divorce their husbands, but only if the husband was sexually immoral.

But it is generally accepted that Mark was written before Matthew, and if that is the case, Mark could not have relied on the fact that Matthew would include that teaching. In any case, both passages in Matthew 19 and Mark 10 make it perfectly clear that Jesus was asked about *husbands* divorcing their *wives*—it was the question he was asked. It was the question he answered, it was the hot topic of the day—could a husband really divorce his wife for *any cause*?

In contrast, there was no dispute about a wife's grounds for divorce. Both the Graeco-Roman and Jewish marriage contracts contemporary to New Testament times that have survived demonstrate a legally binding commitment on the husband to provide for his wife. A similar understanding is demonstrated across the Ancient Near East from as early as 2000 BCE. And as we have seen, the right to divorce if such a provision is not forthcoming is clearly taught in the Bible (§3.5).

It is thus extremely unlikely that Jesus's audience would have assumed in his conversation with the Pharisees that a husband's exception clause, 'except for sexual immorality' was now to be a wife's (only) grounds for divorce, and it is certain that Mark would not have imagined them making that assumption. It would mean that in the one sentence he wrote in his Gospel, he thought that his readership would assume an implicit inclusion of the husband's exception clause in a wife's grounds for divorce, and assume a simultaneous implicit exclusion of her own grounds for divorce as outlined in Exodus 21. It is an understanding that relies on a presumption that his readership would make two assumptions, both of which involve a remarkable about turn in first century ethics in Jewish Palestine.

Furthermore, it would mean that Jesus's teaching as recorded by Mark was different from Mark's own marital imagery, and incompatible with the marital imagery of the rest of the New Testament. All the Gospel writers, including Mark, portray Jesus as the Bridegroom Messiah (e.g. Mark 2:19–20). This marital imagery, as elsewhere in the New Testament, was rooted in contemporary marital practices that were based on the understanding of marriage in ancient Israel, where a husband had a duty to provide for his wife, and any repudiation of him by her was to be based on his failure to do so.

Indeed, because in Mark 10 wives are now addressed separately, he is underlining the fact that they had not been included in Jesus's immediately preceding comments—furthermore, it is difficult to make sense of Jesus's words as recorded if a wife could not initiate a divorce.

This statement in Mark comprises the entire divorce teaching in the Gospels from a wife's perspective. There are two possible interpretations:

1. The statement by Jesus in Mark 10:12 stands as it is written. In effect Jesus removes any Old Testament teaching about divorces initiated by the wife; whatever their previous position, divorce for them is now forbidden.

2. A general principle was being articulated (as in Matthew 19:4–6 and Mark 10:5–9), but the accepted grounds for divorce for wives, taught in Exodus 21, and evidenced in all the marriage contracts dating from that time, were retained even though not, in this context, specifically mentioned.

Most traditional interpretations of the Bible's divorce and remarriage believe, based on Jesus's brief comments, that the Old Testament is swept aside and all gender distinctions are lost. But Jesus did not revoke the Old Testament position—he did not change the accepted teaching. Instead, he brought the Pharisees back to their own Scripture, the Hebrew Bible (our Old Testament), and clarified the position that men could only divorce their wives for sexual impurity.

The assumption of gender reciprocity (i.e. what applies to wives applies to husbands) in New Testament divorce teaching by many that hold the traditional views, in effect, means that Jesus was denying wives their historical divorce rights and greatly restricting their freedom by binding them more firmly to their husbands. It is clear, as we have seen, that under the Old Testament teaching a wife already had divorce grounds that were more broadly based than those of her husband.

Thus I suggest that Mark 10:12, in giving us a general principle for wives, rather than forbidding a wife a divorce, was in fact acknowledging the existence of wife-initiated divorces as evidenced in contemporary Jewish society. However, in this exchange with the Pharisees, the wife's grounds for initiating a divorce were not outlined, almost certainly because that was not the question Jesus was asked—the teaching of Exodus 21 was never in dispute.[52]

The alternative interpretation would mean that Jesus is repudiating that historical teaching, leaving a wife with no means of divorce, a position that it will be seen would appear to contradict the teaching of 1 Corinthians 7— and furthermore, it would mean that the understanding of marriage and divorce would now not match the marital imagery that the New Testament writers, including Mark, employ.

7.10 Summary

Many today hold the view that these short Gospel accounts teach that each marriage was a bond created by God, one that is modelled on Adam and Eve, and that Moses's divorce law was cancelled, at least for Christians. From the analysis above I hope it can be seen that none of these things are supported by a careful exegesis of the text, and certainly not when its context is considered. As seen in chapter 1, to understand Scripture we must evaluate it in its own context before we look to apply it today.

Throughout ancient Israel's history marriage was seen as modelled on Genesis 2:24, not the primal couple, and understood to be a volitional, asymmetrical, conditional, but nonetheless solemn, contractual commitment. For Jesus to make a dramatic change to this understanding he, and the Gospel writers, would have needed to specifically address these issues, not leave them to be deduced from one polemical exchange about divorce with the Pharisees, and two other isolated comments, one in Matthew 5:31–32, and one in Luke 16:18.

When Jesus taught that husbands can only divorce their wives for sexual indecency, he was simply reaffirming Old Testament teaching, and clarifying the Jewish case law on marriage that had, in New Testament times, become the subject of a dispute. Such an analysis is derived from a straightforward exegesis of the text—the Gospel accounts stand as they are written. In contrast, the traditional views read into that Gospel teaching an assumption that wives had the same grounds for divorce as the husband. But this is not taught anywhere in the Bible. It is an unbiblical assumption which repudiates Old Testament teaching and is contrary to both the social context and the Bible's marital imagery that runs from Genesis to Revelation.

By way of contrast, it is safe to assume that the New Testament audience would have understood the Exodus 21 exception clause for a wife divorcing her husband. Unlike the exception clause given for wives by many who hold the traditional views, this exception clause is taught in the Bible (Exodus 21:10–11), and is clearly evidenced historically in Israel, and in contemporary New Testament society. The wife was always free to leave her husband in ancient Israel right through to New Testament times. As we have seen (§3.2), this teaching formed the basis of the Jewish case law on marriage. Jesus when giving the general principle, 'no divorce'—did not cancel a wife's right to do so. And, what is more, Jesus's comment does not make sense unless a wife could initiate a divorce of her husband.

And it must be remembered that the marital imagery underlines this understanding. God would not desert his people unless they were unfaithful to him, but Israel was never compelled to remain in the relationship with him (§4.9). And I think we can see the same concept taught in the New Testament. Paul says in 2 Timothy:

> Therefore I endure everything for the sake of the elect, that they also may obtain the salvation that is in Christ Jesus with eternal glory. The saying is trustworthy, for: If we have died with him, we will also live with him; if we endure, we will also reign with him; if we deny him, he also will deny us; if we are faithless, he remains faithful— for he cannot deny himself. (2 Timothy 2:10–13)

As we saw in §5.5, Paul is saying that Jesus, as our bridegroom, will only breach the betrothal agreement he has with us if we actively 'deny him'—but if we have merely lost faith that he would fulfil his promise to come for us, he would nonetheless be true to that promise. This is consistent with the understanding of an asymmetrical gender-based marriage covenant where a man could only initiate a divorce, or break a betrothal agreement, based on any 'indecency' by his wife/fiancée.

———————————————

Some key points

1. Genesis 2:24 when cited in the New Testament does not represent Adam and Eve's marriage.

2. Jesus was not introducing a new concept of marriage or divorce.

3. The Gospels' teaching on marriage and divorce does not add to, or contradict, the Old Testament teaching.

4. A biblical divorce is when the asymmetrical gender-based roles that form the basis of the marriage agreement are broken.

Some questions

1. How likely do you think it is, as the traditional views suggest, that Jesus overturned the Old Testament teaching, and millennia of divorce practice, in just one short exchange with the Pharisees?

2. Do you think that the *brevity* of the teaching on divorce and remarriage in the Gospels is significant in and of itself?

Chapter 8: Divorce and Remarriage in 1 Corinthians 7

8.1   Introduction

Many believe that Paul in 1 Corinthians 7 adds to what Jesus taught in Matthew 19 and Mark 10 and gives new grounds for divorce—desertion by an unbeliever. This understanding seems to have been derived from the Church of Rome's teaching (called the 'Pauline privilege') that the marriage of those within the communion of the church has a special status, but if either partner in a marriage is not a baptised Roman Catholic, then such a marriage is invalid and can be terminated, even without a divorce.[53]

However, even though Paul is addressing a church in the Graeco-Roman world, it will be argued in this chapter that his own mindset, his own understanding of marriage, was rooted in the Old Testament. Thus I hope to show that in 1 Corinthians 7 Paul outlines the practical outworking of the Old Testament divorce and remarriage teaching for the church age—a teaching that is consonant with both Jesus's teaching in the Gospels, and with the Bible's marital imagery. And although it will be seen that Paul does introduce new teaching ('mixed' marriages are equally as valid as 'non-mixed' marriages, and the Deuteronomy 24 certificate/levirate marriage obligations no longer apply)—he does not give any new grounds for divorce.

8.2   Separation and Divorce

In the first verses of 1 Corinthians 7 the mutual obligations of marriage are addressed, with several scholars seeing a direct link in vv. 3–5 to the triad of obligations for the husband outlined in Exodus 21:10.[54] After a comment regarding the single and widows, Paul addresses the issue of separation/desertion and divorce in vv. 10–16. In the ancient world there was often no formal registration of a marriage—if a marriage partner simply left the marital home it would be deemed a divorce. Consequently, although translations use 'separate' and 'divorce' throughout 1 Corinthians 7, it is not safe to read too much into them—there were more than fifty words used for 'divorce' in contemporary Greek marriage and divorce contracts, and it was common to use several in a single document.

1 Corinthians 7:10–11 has:

> To the married I give this charge (not I, but the Lord): the wife should
> not separate from her husband (but if she does, she should remain
> unmarried or else be reconciled to her husband), and the husband
> should not divorce his wife.

Paul ('not I, but the Lord') here applies the same principle as Jesus in
Matthew 19:4–6 and Mark 10:5–9. When God created the institution of
marriage, divorce was not the intention; so Paul says neither partner should
initiate a separation/divorce—if they have, they should seek a reconciliation.
However, this does not mean that if the separated partner had remarried that
Paul would suggest that the second marriage should be terminated in order
to reinstate the first marriage (see §9.7.2).

8.3   Mixed Marriages

Jesus had not addressed the position on 'mixed' marriages, and it is possible
that the Corinthians had specifically asked Paul a question about them when
they had written to him (v. 1). It will be argued here that Paul teaches that
the Old Testament understanding about such marriages does not apply in
the church era, but that the Old Testament teaching about divorce does.
However, he begins in verses 12–14 by pressing home the 'no divorce'
principle:

> To the rest I say (I, not the Lord) that if any brother has a wife who
> is an unbeliever, and she consents to live with him, he should not
> divorce her. If any woman has a husband who is an unbeliever, and
> he consents to live with her, she should not divorce him. For the
> unbelieving husband is made holy because of his wife, and the
> unbelieving wife is made holy because of her husband. Otherwise
> your children would be unclean, but as it is, they are holy.

This might have seemed a surprising position for Paul to take when the
teaching in Israel (Deuteronomy 23:2) was that, 'No one born of a forbidden
union may enter the assembly of the LORD. Even to the tenth generation,
none of his descendants may enter the assembly of the LORD'—and Ezra's
instruction to the men of Judah had been to divorce their non-Jewish wives
(Ezra 10:11). But there is an important distinction to make between ancient

Israel and the church. In Israel, you were accepted as being Jewish because you were descended from Jacob—your Jewishness was primarily about your blood relationship to him, not about your personal faith in God. A mixed marriage in Israel was not an unbeliever with a believer, but a person with non-Jewish blood married to a Jew—any children they had were considered, in effect, 'unclean' and were not accepted into the congregation.

Some understand from vv. 12–14 that Paul is teaching that the children of mixed-faith marriages, and thus by deduction, the children of all Christians are, in some way, special to God. But Paul is instead saying that those Old Testament principles, whereby children of mixed marriages are excluded from the congregation, do not come through to the Christian faith community.

The children of mixed-faith marriages in the church are 'holy' (v. 14), that is, *not* 'unclean,' and are to be accepted on the same basis as any other children—whether of believers or unbelievers. Paul is here saying that mixed marriages are valid marriages in the faith community, thus any exegesis of the rest of the chapter that understands they are less valid than non-mixed marriages should, I suggest, be treated with caution.

In v. 15 Paul gives a qualification to his principle of 'no separation' that he gave in vv. 10–14:

> But if the unbelieving partner separates, let it be so. In such cases the brother or sister is not enslaved. God has called you to peace.

Some have argued that with his 'not enslaved' (NIV has 'not bound') Paul does not necessarily mean that a divorce is possible. But contemporary divorce documents that have survived show that this very same terminology is used to declare that the marital obligations are terminated—in other words they are, in effect, the certificates as required in Deuteronomy 24 to show that the divorced wife is free to remarry (§3.5). Paul would have *avoided* using the terminology 'not bound' if he was *not* talking about a divorce.

His argument is following the same path as Matthew 19:3–9, where Jesus first gave the general principle of no divorce, then followed it with his divorce teaching. It is not generally thought that in Matthew 19 Jesus is contradicting himself, and there is no need to believe that Paul is doing so in this chapter. When he gives his general principle in vv. 10–14, he is not contradicting any Gospel divorce teaching, or the teaching of Exodus 21:10–11 and Deuteronomy 24:1–4, where it is clear a wife or a husband (with no reference to their personal faith) can initiate a divorce—because in v. 15 he acknowledges that the reconciliation he suggests in v. 11 might not be possible, and in such a situation he recommends: 'let it be so.'

It is possible that Paul wanted to address the subject because he realised mixed marriages would be vulnerable. Desertion is more likely to happen if one partner is an unbeliever. But the key issue Paul is teaching is about desertion, not the personal faith (or lack of it) of the partner. Jesus had not specifically addressed this issue, he was not asked about it, it was not a controversial subject. Paul simply reaffirms the historical biblical position. His teaching that desertion is divorce for any marriage, mixed or otherwise, is fully in accord with the Old Testament understanding (and that of the wider Ancient Near East). However, most believe that because Paul talks about desertion in the context of mixed marriages, it only applies in that context but as Craig Blomberg comments:

> desertion was Paul's primary concern; that it was an unbeliever wanting to leave is "accidental" in the technical sense of that term.... Once again, in an age and culture in which divorce almost universally carried with it provisions for remarriage, Paul would have had specifically to exclude this possibility in v. 15 if he had expected anyone to understand that he was actually forbidding all remarriage.[55]

Perhaps an illustration might help us understand Blomberg's observation. Imagine setting out on a car journey and saying to your travelling companions, 'I have had some trouble with that tyre—it must have a slow puncture.' Then one of the group says, 'If it goes down we must change it.' Of course, it is not intended to mean that if a different tyre goes down that that one will not be changed. The observation was about a vulnerable tyre, whereas the principle understood was that any punctured tyre would be changed. Paul's teaching applies to desertion in any marriage—not just the potentially vulnerable 'mixed' marriages to which vv. 12–14 refer.

Although Scripture is against mixed-faith marriages in the community of God's people (e.g. Deuteronomy 7:1–4; 1 Corinthians 7:39; 2 Corinthians 6:14) there is not a concept that such a marriage is in some way not valid as a marriage. When Jesus was asked about divorce he is recorded as referencing the creation ordinance of marriage, not any ethnic or faith community to find its *raison d'etre*—marriage was intended for all people, not made valid (or more valid) by the personal faith of one or both spouses.

As mentioned in §8.1, the logic of different rules for marriages where one partner is an unbeliever appears to be rooted in the Roman Catholic understanding of marriage—it is a teaching that survived the Reformation and has been widely accepted within the Christian community. But while such marriages might be more vulnerable, they are not less valid.

Thus, while both mixed marriages and non-mixed marriages are valid marriages, it might be considered that the expectations of the latter would be greater, and that any separation/divorce in the marriage of two believers would be based on biblical grounds. Nonetheless, Paul teaches in v. 15 that if a marriage partner has been abandoned by their spouse, whatever the personal faith of either of them, they can take that to be a divorce and are free to remarry (notwithstanding, they must fulfill any obligations for state-registered marriages).

8.4   Not Bound

There was a potential problem for any wife in ancient Israel, in that while she could initiate a divorce, she needed the divorce certificate from her husband that stated that she was now 'not bound.' She was similarly bound if her husband had separated from her without first giving her the certificate. This meant, that although the couple were separated and to all intents and purposes divorced, the wife was still bound to her husband in that she was unable to remarry until she received the certificate, or the death of her husband had been proven—the rabbis going to some length to determine what counted as such before the woman was allowed to remarry.[56] It is a problem that still exists in Israel today, and in Jewish faith communities in other nations. If a couple decide to separate/divorce, and the husband refuses to release his wife by issuing a divorce certificate she is, as the Jewish community describes it, *agunah* ('chained').

In contrast, Paul says in v. 15 that on desertion neither 'brother or sister is bound,' and as I outline above (§8.3), Paul is saying that the deserted partner, if a reconciliation is not possible, is free to remarry. The wife's freedom to divorce in v. 15 is fully compatible with the *qal va-chomer* (light to heavy) argument from the situation outlined in Exodus 21, where even a slave woman was not 'enslaved' to her husband — but what *is* new, is that it seems clear that Paul is cancelling the requirement for the Deuteronomy 24 certificate for the church age. Accordingly, there is today no concept of *agunah* in the Christian church.

If it is thought that any freedom taught by Paul applies only to those in mixed marriages, it would mean that with his '*not* enslaved,' Paul was introducing a new form of 'enslavement' for a husband who had been deserted by his Christian wife — since under the Old Testament teaching, a husband had no need of a certificate and would have always been free to remarry. Furthermore, this new 'enslavement' is to be based on the profession of faith of a wife who was no longer with him, and indeed with whom he might have no further contact. How would he know if she still maintained a profession of faith? Those traditional views that believe Paul is saying a Christian couple are bound, but if one partner is not a Christian they are not bound, attribute to him a teaching that has so many novel aspects about it that he would have had to explain more fully what he was saying.

In contrast, I suggest it is easy to follow the logic of Paul's argument. If the woman had been deserted, her husband was clearly not providing her with her entitlement, and although she had not received her certificate as outlined in Deuteronomy 24:1–4, she could, 'for the sake of peace,' consider herself divorced and free to remarry. Furthermore, Paul seems to be saying that the husband could assume that a deserting wife was in effect divorcing him, so he should release her without evidence of sexual impurity — such teaching is consonant both with Exodus 21:10–11, and with the all the Bible's marital imagery, in that God's 'wife' and Jesus's 'bride' are free to go — neither are held against their will. Paul's cancellation of the requirement for a Deuteronomy 24 certificate acknowledges that the gospel is not confined to national Israel, and that other nation states might legitimately introduce different procedures (not grounds) for handling divorce and remarriage — or indeed, have none at all.

In summary, Paul's 'no divorce' principle must not be forgotten in any application of his 'not bound' teaching—but to deny remarriage to any deserted marriage partner goes against the Bible's understanding of marriage and divorce as revealed in its legislation, its narratives, and its marital imagery.

8.5   Remarriage after Widowhood

Paul goes to remarriage teaching again at the end of the chapter:

> A wife is bound to her husband as long as he lives. But if her husband dies, she is free to be married to whom she wishes, only in the Lord. Yet in my judgment she is happier if she remains as she is. And I think that I too have the Spirit of God. (1 Corinthians 7:39–40)

If taken out of context the statement that, 'A wife is bound to her husband as long as he lives' would mean Paul would not only be contradicting the teaching of Jesus in Matthew, he would be contradicting what he himself had just said—that is, a wife is *not* bound when a separation/divorce has occurred. Instead, Paul is here making a point about widows, and after stating his general principle (a wife is bound to her husband as long as he lives), he says that on her husband's death she is free to remarry whoever she wants, provided he is a Christian.

Although it might seem obvious that a widow can marry whoever she wants, in the Old Testament there was what is known as the levirate obligation for a widow to marry her deceased husband's brother (Deuteronomy 25:5–10). This was, at least in part, a reflection of the understanding of marriage in Israel that when a woman became a man's wife she belonged to her new family and they had an ongoing duty to her beyond the death of her husband. Paul is here freeing widows in the church age from any obligation to marry within their deceased husband's family.

8.6   Summary

Paul's teaching in this chapter is in line with both the marriage teaching and marital imagery found elsewhere in both the Old Testament and the New Testament. He teaches that desertion by either partner is grounds for divorce. It has been seen that a wife was free to initiate a divorce from her husband if she believed she was not being provided for (Exodus 21:10–11)—thus any desertion by her would indicate such, and would amount to a divorce. If a husband deserted his wife he would obviously be failing in his duties, and the wife would be free to consider it a divorce—thus Paul, was in effect, in this chapter, applying the teaching of Exodus 21:10–11.

The subject of desertion, or mixed marriages, did not arise in the Gospels—it seems Jesus was not asked about them. So Paul clarified the biblical teaching about desertion for the Corinthians in the context of mixed marriages—it is very probably a question they had raised (v. 1). In so doing he gave a new teaching that would have surprised many of his Jewish contemporaries—it was that mixed marriages were valid marriages (*contra* the historical understanding in Judaism) and should, if at all possible, be maintained. It is ironic that many traditional views today teach, in effect, the opposite of what Paul taught—that is, that mixed marriages are not as valid as marriages between two believers.

But no new grounds for initiating a divorce are given in 1 Corinthians 7 to either the husband or the wife. Although the chapter expresses the ideal of mutual commitment (vv. 3–5, 33–34), these commitments are not the same as the grounds for divorce. In other words, only the failure to fulfil certain specific (asymmetrical) expectations are given as grounds for initiating a divorce in Scripture. Thus there is no such thing as the 'Pauline privilege' in the chapter—Paul was merely explaining the logic of the biblical position to the Corinthian church. If Paul was looking to convey the concept that grounds for initiating a divorce in the New Testament era were to be based on a wider range of marital expectations, it might be thought he would have endeavoured to express it as clearly as possible. The understanding of divorce in the Old Testament, and across the Ancient Near East had not changed for millennia—it is a teaching that both Jesus and Paul affirmed.

Throughout the recorded history of ancient Israel marriage is demonstrated to be a volitional, conditional, asymmetrical, affinity covenant—and this understanding is consonant with all the Bible's marital imagery. Divorce was to be based on the failure to fulfil those specific covenantal obligations. For example, although Deuteronomy 10:12 states that Israel had a duty to love their God, the Old Testament does not seem anywhere to mention Israel's love for him. But God's divorce of Israel was not for their lack of love for him, nor was it for their failure to meet any expectations which he may have had in terms of wider covenant obedience, but for the sole reason that they had forsaken him and behaved as 'prostitutes.' The same can be seen in 2 Timothy 2:10–13, where Christ will only breach his betrothal promise if believers 'deny' him—not because of a lack of sufficient love for him (see §5.5).

We saw in §7.2 that when Jesus taught that husbands can only divorce their wives for sexual indecency he was simply reaffirming Old Testament teaching and clarifying the Jewish case law on marriage that had, in New Testament times, become the subject of a dispute. Here in 1 Corinthians 7, Paul explains how the Jewish case law based on Exodus 21:10–11 applies to the Christian church—he gives no new divorce grounds. But he does give new teaching: mixed marriages in the faith community are valid marriages (vv. 12–14); after a divorce a wife does not need a certificate from her husband to remarry (v. 15); and a widow is free to marry who she wants, 'only in the Lord' (v. 39).

In chapter 9 we shall consider whether the gender-based divorce grounds in the Old Testament law of marriage that formed the basis of Jesus and Paul's teaching are relevant today when, in much of the developed world, there is greater social and economic equality between marriage partners.

———————————

Some key points

1. Paul reaffirms the biblical teaching about desertion in the context of mixed marriages.

2. Paul's teaching is based on the fact that he sees a mixed marriage in Judaism is different to a mixed marriage in the church age.

3. There are no new divorce grounds in 1 Corinthians 7—there is no Pauline privilege.

4. But Paul does give three new teachings for the church age.

Some questions

1. In light of this chapter, can you explain what Paul means in 1 Corinthians 7:14, and how that differs from what many Christians believe today about the children of believers?

2. Can you think of some of the pastoral problems inherent in the traditional views that say a Christian deserted by an unbeliever can divorce and remarry, but if deserted by a believer, they cannot?

3. Can you list Paul's three new teachings?

Chapter 9: Pastoral Realities

9.1   Introduction

This book has hopefully demonstrated that the Bible's teaching on divorce and remarriage is both clear and consistent.

It is clear, in that the Old Testament demonstrates that ancient Israel based their marriage and divorce teaching on Exodus 21:10–11 and Deuteronomy 24:1–4 (§3.2; §3.5). It is a teaching endorsed by Jesus and Paul. Deuteronomy 24:1–4 is specifically affirmed by Jesus in Matthew 5 and 19 (§7), and Paul in 1 Corinthians 7 applies the principles of Exodus 21:10–11 for the church age (§8). The sole purpose of the husband's certificate of divorce, as required in Deuteronomy 24, was to allow remarriage. The Old Testament position was that any valid divorce permits a remarriage, and nothing that the New Testament teaches contradicts that (see analysis in §7.5). Indeed, Paul goes further, and in 1 Corinthians 7:15 frees a divorced wife from the need of a certificate (§8.4), and in v. 39, he frees a widow from the levirate obligation (§8.5).

The Bible's divorce and remarriage teaching is also consistent, in that the New Testament teaches the same as the Old Testament, and all the key features of the *Divine Marriage*, God 'married'/'betrothed' to his people, are mirrored in the Bible's teaching about human marriage. The Bible's teaching also demonstrates an external consistency, in that it is consonant with the understanding of marriage and divorce that is demonstrated in ancient Israel through to New Testament times.

Despite the Bible's clarity and consistency, it does not address every possible scenario—often it is necessary to fall back on broader biblical principles to decide how to act in any contemporary situation. Any analysis/advice given here is done so with humility—ultimately, anybody with pastoral responsibilities counselling a couple must exercise their own judgement and, as Scripture teaches, ask God for wisdom (James 1:5).

9.2   Defining Marriage

As we have seen, the Old Testament narratives often point to family involvement in the formation of a marriage, but there is no stated definition of marriage in Scripture, nor is there any agreed ceremony or verbal formula that would make a couple 'married.' Furthermore, in ancient Israel marriages were not registered with the state, or under the control of the priesthood. Nonetheless, it is clear that marriage was perceived to be a committed, exclusive, hetero-sexual relationship, and recognised as such in the community.

The early post-apostolic church developed a neoplatonic understanding of marriage (§1.6), from which came the Roman Catholic Church belief that marriage was a sacrament (that is, something was thought to happen in heaven on marriage). As a consequence, they taught that marriage was to be performed by a priest according to a set liturgy.

In the 16th century the Reformers on the continent came to understand marriage as a creation ordinance, rather than a sacrament, and for the first-time marriage was considered to be the responsibility of the state. However, in England, marriage was not transferred from the church to the state until the middle of the 19th century.

Today, many Christians, perhaps unaware of this history, consider that nobody is 'married' unless they *are* married by the state. Although for many years the societal norm has been for couples to register their relationship with the state, there was never a requirement to do so, and many today do not. And certainly we cannot point to any Bible teaching that suggests that they must. Notwithstanding that, any particular fellowship might insist that members who are considering marriage adhere to certain protocols (for example, a formal ceremony) if that is considered the societal norm within the culture they operate. But the question is: Should we insist on enforcing such when we counsel others?

Perhaps an illustration of just one hypothetical situation will highlight the potential pastoral problem in this area:

Megan and Jack

Megan lives locally and is not a believer but has started attending your church with her two young children. She has been with Jack for more than 10 years, they have had the children together, but are now having marital difficulties. A church member, while counselling the couple, says that as there had been no ceremony, formal engagement, or state registration of the relationship, in the view of their church, they are not married. Megan is upset to think that the church sees their relationship as being immoral and no longer attends. Jack now feels less obligated to the relationship and leaves.

Thus I suggest that it is pastorally expedient to treat any hetero-sexual couple that see themselves as married, or are in a long term committed relationship (that is, not casual co-habitation), as being married, even if they have not been through any of the traditional marriage protocols. As evangelicals, when we preach the gospel, we usually separate its requirements from cultural norms. But more importantly for this chapter, it seems that pastoral wisdom points to that conclusion.

9.3   Getting Married

Perhaps there would be less marital breakdown if before a couple married more time was spent in counselling about the respective roles of the husband and wife in marriage, according to the Bible. Ideally, in light of that teaching, both partners should express clearly what they expect from each other. Too often couples contemplating marriage are asked to 'seek the Lord's will,' which for many means trying to interpret providential signposts, but there is no clear teaching in the Bible to suggest that this is the way forward (see reference to Isaac and Rebekah in §3.3).

Often a couple say they want to marry because they are in love. But this focus on romantic love is a later Western development, and although love as an emotion is obviously a factor in marriage, in biblical teaching it is not the essence of it. The biblical emphasis is on love as an action. In the New Testament there are more than 200 verses that contain the word love and its cognates, but there are only three passages that refer to love between a husband and a wife—and they all use love as a verb.[57] In other words, in the Bible, marital love is primarily a required action, not an emotion.

If either party to the proposed marriage had been married before it would certainly be wise to ask the circumstances in which their previous marriage ended—see §9.9 and §9.10 below. Second marriages, especially those that have children from previous relationships, can bring their own problems. It is not a sign of failure to admit that such is beyond the counselling skills within your own fellowship and to seek help elsewhere.

However, it is beyond the scope of this chapter to deal with the principles of marriage, or any counselling issues for those either having marital difficulties or coping with the aftermath of a divorce. There are many books available that cover these matters. The focus here is to try and address the pastoral issues that might occur when trying to apply the biblical teaching about divorce and remarriage in a local fellowship.

9.4   Some Pastoral Principles for Divorce

Both Jesus in the Gospels, and Paul in 1 Corinthians 7, start their teaching on divorce with the principle, 'no divorce.' And Paul says even if there has been a separation, a reconciliation should be sought. That clear principle should not be lost sight of in the ensuing discussion in this chapter. A first duty of any counsellor is to make every effort to maintain the marriage and keep the couple together if that can be done at all in a God-honouring way.

The second duty is to decide whether the divorce is valid, without trying to allocate 'guilt' or 'innocence.' The question to be addressed is: Has any behaviour given rise to there being valid grounds for divorce? That is the question we are considering in this chapter. Church discipline is a separate issue. It is up to the spiritual oversight of a church to decide what action to take in the case of any perceived sinful behaviour by a church member. Such action might be to do nothing at all, to exercise some form of church discipline, or in extreme cases, to excommunicate the offender from the fellowship, as is described in Matthew 18:15–18, and as Paul recommends in 1 Corinthians 5.

A third duty is to follow the example of our Lord and err on the side of grace and love—in other words, to remember to treat any couple with love and respect even if they do not align themselves with our own understanding of marriage; to remember that marriage was made for man, not man for marriage (see §9.5 below); and to bear in mind Paul's call to peace (1 Corinthians 7:15).

As with any counselling, when you have explained the biblical principles, in the end, it is up to the couple themselves what they do. If any couple choose to divorce (and go on to a new marriage) that is their decision. In the Genesis account, we are told God created man in his image and gave him the autonomy to make decisions—even though he might not (and did not) approve of all those choices.

With any divorce, whether or not a couple have registered their relationship with the state, there could be legal and financial issues to handle which might involve recourse to a lawyer—even if both parties are Christians and it is an amicable divorce. But in this chapter, we are only considering how the biblical teaching relates to the couple themselves and the fellowship they are part of.

9.5   Gender Based Divorce Grounds: Are they for Today?

In Matthew 19 and Mark 10 the Pharisees asked Jesus about an 'any cause' divorce for husbands. In reply Jesus took them back to the teaching of Deuteronomy 24 and clarified the fact that there had to have been sexual immorality on the part of a wife for a husband to be able to initiate a divorce. Moral rules in Scripture apply across all social settings, so we need to decide if Jesus was answering on a moral basis, or whether his teaching was simply to protect wives in the social conditions of Bible times. In other words, can we treat a divorce initiated by the husband as valid in our affluent more socially gender-neutral 21st century Western society, even if the wife has not been sexually immoral?

The answer to that question might be influenced by what we think of the Bible's marital imagery. We have seen something of the key role that is played by the imagery in telling the story of our salvation. There are possibly two viewpoints:

1. The Old Testament writers used the technique of imagining that God was 'married' to Israel as a helpful way of portraying his relationship to them. The gender-based marital relationships happened to suit their purposes.

2. God designed marriage from the beginning to portray the drama of a heavenly reality—the nature of his own being, the loss of his special creation (Adam), the rescue plan he would mount in Christ, and the relationship of his people to himself in the period in between the Garden of Eden and the new Eden in heaven.

I am persuaded that the second viewpoint is correct. This would suggest that the biblical gender roles in marriage were given to serve a higher purpose, and were not just about protecting women. Nonetheless, we must bear in mind, that as well as being a picture of God's relationship to his people, marriage was for our benefit. Genesis 2:18 says, 'Then the LORD God said, "It is not good that the man should be alone; I will make him a helper fit for him."' Just as the Sabbath was made for man, not man for the Sabbath (Mark 2:27), so marriage was made for our benefit, not that we were made for marriage.

And we have to face pastoral realities. A marriage might have irretrievably broken down but the wife, who has been sexually faithful, wants to remain married. In that case, is there no way forward for the husband with a valid divorce? We might in this circumstance need to consider the concept of the 'lesser of two evils' (e.g. Exodus 1:15–20)—in other words, which path will cause least harm? Paul seems to invoke this concept in 1 Corinthians 7:15 in his call to peace. His comment reflects a rabbinic argument, that when a solution cannot be found according to law, then the guiding principle should be to look for peace.

Putting these things together, I do not think we must label every such divorce as invalid, and thereby imply that any remarriage would not be endorsed by the church. In the Christian life, there are not always simple answers to every question. Anybody with pastoral responsibilities is duty bound before God to get to the best understanding as possible of Scripture, and then to act with wisdom and compassion in the situation they are presented with.

9.6 Valid and Invalid Divorces

For many familiar with traditional divorce teaching perhaps the most difficult biblical concept to grasp is that the Bible's teaching about the validity of a divorce and any remarriage is not based on guilt or innocence. The sole issue is this: is the divorce valid? If it is, then remarriage is valid — for both partners. And we should note that our holy God, who is without sin, divorced Israel. It was a valid divorce. A valid divorce is not *in and of itself* sinful.

Also, it is important to remember that while a divorce might be valid, it does not mean it is necessary. God endured centuries of waywardness with Israel before finally exiling them in 722 BCE. There is no Scripture teaching that compels a divorce based on there being a valid case for such — excepting in Ezra 10:11 where there is an instruction to those Jews who had married non-Jewish women to divorce their wives. Those divorces were based on ethnicity, and such divorce grounds do not come through to the faith community, as Paul teaches in 1 Corinthians 7 (see §8.3).

There are three valid grounds for initiating a divorce given in Scripture:

1. The wife is not provided for sufficiently by her husband.

2. There has been sexual immorality by the wife.

3. Desertion by the husband or the wife.

As we have seen, marriage is a creation ordinance (§8.3), and although many of the traditional views teach differently, in Scripture, it is clear that these divorce grounds apply to all humanity regardless of the personal faith of either spouse. Another difficulty for those of us more familiar with the traditional views, is to accept that a wife is free to initiate a divorce based on a lack of provision by her husband, the first of these three grounds for divorce. But there are four powerful arguments to support it. Firstly, it is plainly taught in Exodus 21, which as we have seen, forms the basis of Paul's teaching in 1 Corinthians 7. Secondly, the wife's entitlement to the Exodus triad, written into all the Jewish marriage contracts that have been found contemporary to New Testament times, suggests that failure in such by the husband would be a breach of contract.[58]

Thirdly, it is embedded in the Bible's marital imagery, in that the 'wife' in the *Divine Marriage* can leave that marriage at any time of her own volition. In other words, this is the basis of God's own understanding of marriage. Who could say God's provision for Israel was not adequate'? Yet she was nonetheless free to leave him—she was 'not enslaved' (1 Corinthians 7:15). And although through Joshua he pleaded with her to stay (Joshua 24), he never prevented her leaving, or suggested any reprisals if she did, except that she would lose his provision and protection (Israel is portrayed as regretting such in Hosea 2:7–9).

And nobody is forced against their will either to come to Christ, or remain with him. We are drawn to Christ as the Spirit regenerates us and causes us to choose him (John 3:1–8). Our ongoing security with Christ is guaranteed by our circumcised hearts (the hallmark of every true believer), which mean we will never choose to leave him—thus we are safe in his hands (Jeremiah 31:33; Romans 2:29; John 10:28–30).

And fourthly, it is widely taught in evangelical circles that a wife is subject to her husband, so if she did not have freedom to leave the marriage, she would be less free than the slave wife described in Exodus 21. So specific Scripture teaching, the known world of New Testament times, the Bible's pervasive marital imagery, and the logic of a wife's submission to her husband, all speak with one voice—the wife is to be released from the marriage if she wants it. In other words, a divorce initiated by a wife is to be treated as a valid divorce.

Whether any divorce initiated by a wife for lack of provision of her needs *is* valid or not is another issue. Exodus 21:10 speaks of food, clothes, and marital rights (and that seems to include her emotional needs, §3.2)—I suggest that these 'marital rights' are not capable of objective assessment. Only she can know if such have been met. Certainly, there is not in Scripture any specific criteria given as to what constitutes sufficient provision. Although this did not deter the rabbis from drawing up such lists—including a schedule for a husband's conjugal duties based on his employment status.[59]

Several have told me they are not convinced that a wife should be free to decide if she is, or is not, sufficiently provided for. When I ask who else might decide, it has been suggested to me the pastor, or the husband. But how could the pastor know? How would he be able to accurately assess the wife's sexual and emotional needs? And certainly he would have no basis in Scripture to have any authority to pronounce on it. So perhaps the husband? But if the husband had the authority to decide if he was adequately providing for his wife, he would be, in effect, the accused, the judge, and the jury! The wife's 'freedom' would be meaningless.

For all these reasons, in the end, only the wife (and God) knows—so the matter is between her and God. It follows that the pastoral reality is that if a wife is determined to have a divorce, it is difficult, and I suggest ultimately impossible, for the spiritual oversight of the church to say that her desire for a divorce has no basis, and thus the divorce would be invalid. In Old Testament times these matters were not decided by any priest, prophet, or elder, and no New Testament teaching suggests any different.

In light of this, the only biblical justifiable role for church leaders is to advise on the biblical teaching, and offer counselling—the issue must lie with the couple themselves, and the final decision is for the wife alone.[60] To deny her that is to deny specific Scripture teaching. She can have a valid divorce. But this does not mean that in the view of the oversight of the church a valid divorce is always a justified divorce. Our subject for the moment is not about making judgements about an individual's behaviour, or providing any counselling, we are simply clarifying what counts, in Scripture, as a valid divorce.

Hopefully it can now be seen, at least in pastoral terms, that there can only be one *invalid* divorce—that is when a husband divorces his wife even though there has been no sexual immorality by her. We will now look at various hypothetical practical situations and see if some pointers can be given as to what might be a wise approach.

9.7   Hypothetical Divorce Scenarios

9.7.1   Divorce Involving Sexual Immorality

Alan and Margaret

Margaret has started a lesbian relationship with a girlfriend.

Is this sexual immorality that would justify a divorce by Alan? In §7.5 we looked at the word *porneia*, given as grounds for divorce by a husband in Matthew 5 and 19, usually translated as sexual immorality in our English Bibles (as it is in 1 Corinthians 6:9 and 1 Timothy 1:10) — and saw that there is a certain ambiguity about it. *Porneia* would certainly include adultery, but what about lesbian sex acts by a wife? Such would not technically be adultery if we confined ourselves to the biblical definition — which as we have seen, is a married woman having sexual intercourse with a man who is not her husband.

Scripture spares us a definitive list of the many types of sexual immorality depraved humanity can imagine. But I think most would agree that if a wife performs any sexual act with somebody not her husband, that such would be thought of as sexual immorality, and her husband would have grounds for seeking a divorce.

But what else? There is a strong linguistic argument that the Deuteronomy 24 case law that allowed divorce for 'a matter of indecency' included indecent exposure, and if so, it might be expected to be included in the restatement of that teaching in Matthew 19 when the word *porneia* was used. Thus if a wife was behaving in what was thought by her husband to be an inappropriate sexualised manner, for example, taking a job as a lap dancer, or repeatedly watching pornography — and she persisted in such against his wishes, he might have valid grounds for divorce based on that understanding of the text of Scripture.

Bob and Ruth

Ruth has an affair.

Bob can choose to forgive Ruth, and this should be the first option. But Bob is free to divorce her as Matthew 5:32 and 19:9 explains.

Ken and Lynda

Ken has an affair.

As with Bob above, Lynda can choose to forgive Ken — infidelity does not mean that the marriage is automatically terminated. However, Lynda can initiate a divorce for Ken's sexual unfaithfulness—this is the teaching of Exodus 21:10–11.

Kevin and Jessica

Kevin is addicted to pornography.

Jessica should encourage Kevin to get help with this. But in the end if no resolution is found, and Jessica cannot cope with it, she is free to go.

9.7.2   Divorce Involving Desertion/Separation

Barry and Helen

Are both believers. Helen leaves Barry for another man.

Barry can have a biblical divorce because his wife has chosen to leave him— even if in the minds of some her reason for leaving was not valid. The first line of counselling is to try and get a reconciliation (1 Corinthians 7:10–11), but Helen is entitled to say she does not want such. Barry is free because Helen has initiated a divorce by leaving him. Helen has in any case, because of the subsequent relationship, been sexually unfaithful. This is the teaching of Exodus 21:10–11, Matthew 5:32, and Matthew 19:9.

Bill and Mary

Bill is a believer but Mary isn't. There are difficulties. Mary leaves.

As in any marriage involving desertion, Bill is 'not bound' (1 Corinthians 7:15), he can have a valid divorce.

Darren and Jennifer

Are both believers. Jennifer deserts Darren. No other person is involved.

As with Bill above, Darren is not bound to keep the marriage together. Jennifer has effectively divorced him.

David and Christine

Are both believers. Christine decides she 'does not love David anymore' and leaves him.

Christine has separated from David who everybody perceives to have been a loving husband. David is entitled to assume that Christine is divorcing him. Pastorally, the only realistic path (for the reasons outlined in §9.6 above) would be to treat this as a valid divorce, even if Christine's action appears not to be justified. Who can be sure what David is like in the privacy of the marital home?

Oliver and Hannah

Are both believers and have separated but not divorced. Hannah wants Oliver to come back and points to Paul's exhortation in 1 Corinthians 7:10–11 that separated couples should be reconciled. Oliver, however, has formed a new settled relationship with another woman.

Oliver has, in effect, established a new marriage. Does Paul's teaching apply in this situation? Although Oliver's separation/divorce from Hannah might not have been valid, it does not mean that his new relationship is not a marriage (see §7.7 and §9.10 below). At face value, it does not seem to be wise to suggest a divorce in the second marriage in order to reinstate the first. As with all these examples, I am not addressing the issue of church discipline, which Oliver's behaviour might be thought to justify.

9.7.3   Divorce for Other Reasons

Ed and Clare

Clare has for some time been unhappy in the marriage. She is reluctant to discuss what the problem is with the pastoral oversight of their fellowship and wants a divorce.

As seen above (§9.6), there is no teaching or example in Scripture that gives any third party the right to decide whether or not a wife should be happy with her provision, and certainly not her 'marital rights.' This, in effect, gives the wife the freedom to initiate a divorce on her own terms. Although every attempt should be made to keep Ed and Clare's marriage together, Clare is free to leave, as Exodus 21 specifically teaches.

This is fundamental to all the Bible's marital imagery, where Adam, Israel, Judah, and the church are all portrayed as God's 'wife'—and none are bound to him against their will. Such is the godly pattern for marriage. His people are only 'bound' to him by their desire to be with him based on their love for him (Romans 8:28). In heaven we will be forever with Christ, and surely nobody will be there against their will.

John and Susan

There are many arguments, mostly because Susan wants more material things than John is happy, or able, to provide. In both their minds the marriage has come to the end and they want a divorce. There has been no infidelity and John believes he has been a good husband.

John cannot initiate a valid divorce. Susan for her part must decide if John is providing for her adequately. If she thinks he is, then an attempt should be made to find some way through the problems they have. If Susan believes that John is not sufficiently providing for her — then she can initiate a divorce. Although every effort should be made to get the marriage back on track, if Susan wants to go, she can.

Harry and Anne

There is a history of domestic violence by Harry.

Anne is entitled to the 'marital rights,' as outlined in Exodus 21:10–11, which would include emotional support (§3.2). Physical abuse by Harry would seem to be a clear breach of this entitlement and so she can divorce him.

9.7.4   Invalid Divorces

Lucas and Sophia

Lucas divorces Sophia because he is in love with somebody else. There has been no immorality on Sophia's part.

This would be an invalid divorce.

Michael and Fran

Michael says his marital physical relationship with Fran has never been good and he wants a divorce.

Fran has not been sexually immoral, so this would be an invalid divorce. Any divorce initiated by the husband against the wishes of his wife when there has been no sexual immorality on her part, is a scripturally invalid divorce, as Jesus makes clear in Matthew 5 and 19.

Simon and Emily

There are many arguments about a range of issues. Simon is doing his best, but is increasingly stressed and unhappy, and wants a divorce. Emily however, does not.

It is not for the pastoral oversight to say what Simon can or cannot do. But if Simon decides to divorce Emily, how should the pastoral oversight of their church deal with this? This is a difficult area. When Jesus said that a husband could only initiate a divorce of his wife for her sexual immorality, did he not envisage any other exceptions at all? One of the church fathers (Origen d. 254 CE) pointed out that this means that a wife might have murdered their infant children, and yet a divorce would still not be allowed.

If, even after much counselling with the couple, it was thought that Simon genuinely could not cope with the marriage anymore, then pastoral wisdom might be to say that they would, in their own fellowship, consider this divorce as valid. Such a decision, although not precisely in accord with New Testament teaching, might be thought to be consonant with Paul's call to peace in 1 Corinthians 7:15, and the fact that divorced wives suffer less disadvantage in modern Western culture than in New Testament times.

William and Karen

Karen is often physically abusive to William, he wants a divorce, but Karen does not.

This would be an invalid divorce. The question to be addressed by any church leadership is the same as in Simon and Emily above—can they consider treating a divorce by William in their own fellowship as valid? Again, the implications of Paul's call to peace (1 Corinthians 7:15) would need to carefully considered.

9.8   Remarriage After Divorce

We will look at the principles involved in remarriage after valid and invalid divorces below. As we have seen, such does not involve an assessment of guilt or innocence—but a divorced partner might have feelings of guilt even though their behaviour, at least at face value, had not caused the divorce. There is such a thing as 'godly grief' (2 Corinthians 7:9–10) that has a positive outcome; but in Matthew 23:1–4 Jesus speaks of the Pharisees laying on people unnecessary burdens. It might be advisable for any counsellor to ask the couple if there are any outstanding matters from any previous divorce they would like to discuss before going on to counsel about a planned new marriage.

9.9   Remarriage After a Valid Divorce

A valid divorce means that both the husband and wife are now as single people before God and are free to remarry. But not everything that is legitimate is wise. A valid divorce does not mean that there was no sin. A single man, whether previously married or not, might present himself to be married, but it is known to the church leadership that he has a history of abusive relationships with women. They might choose not to conduct a marriage service for him if they thought it could bring their fellowship into disrepute. But they could not forbid him marriage, or say that any marriage he contracts would be invalid.

Furthermore, a couple might have had a biblically valid divorce, in that the husband initiated a divorce for his wife's unfaithfulness, but the person presenting for remarriage is the unfaithful wife. Here again wisdom by the oversight of the church and knowledge of the individual is required. Presumably the church leadership will look to see if repentance is evidenced and there is a full understanding of the obligations of the new marriage. If the sexual unfaithfulness had occurred within the fellowship it might be wiser to counsel the couple to join another fellowship.

Every situation has to be treated individually. This applies to all couples who want to marry, and especially when it is a remarriage after divorce. Prior knowledge of the parties will inform the counselling, because even when a sexually faithful divorced wife presents for marriage, or a divorced woman who feels she was not provided for in her previous marriage, it cannot be presumed that there was not a pattern of sinful behaviour by her in the previous marriage. But there is nothing *per se* to forbid it.

Let us consider again the case of Ken and Lynda as above (§9.7.1). If Lynda accepts the fact that the marriage is over, it in effect immediately becomes a valid divorce. Why? Because she has declared it to be a divorce. She no longer wants to be the wife of that man. This is the teaching of Exodus 21:10–11 and 1 Corinthians 7, and the logic of all the Bible's marital imagery.

Ken now wants to remarry. He is free to do so—but his church leadership would surely want to discuss the issue with him, and his intended new wife. If there was no evidence of repentance, and no clear indication Ken would not do the same again, even though before God he would be free to remarry, they might choose not to conduct the marriage.

Even if there was repentance, if Lynda (his former wife) was still in the fellowship, it might be suggested that Ken went to a different fellowship. Not because he was sinning in remarrying, but because it might unsettle Lynda. There appears to be a similar principle outlined in Leviticus 20:21 which seems to teach that a man should not marry the wife of his divorced brother. The possible reason for this could be that he would be unsettled to see his ex-wife with his brother (a second reason might be that this law code was intended to discourage potential sexual attraction in affinity relationships within families). A decision would need to be made that is 'according to peace' (1 Corinthians 7:15).

9.10   Remarriage After an Invalid Divorce

But what if Lynda had forgiven Ken, but Ken decides to leave Lynda anyway? This is an invalid divorce. Lynda does not want a divorce, and there has been no sexual immorality on her part.

A straightforward 'black and white' position for a fellowship to take is to not participate in, or recognise, any remarriage after an invalid divorce. But it must be remembered that if the divorce was invalid for one partner it is invalid for both. There is no example, or teaching, anywhere in Scripture, to support the concept that it is possible to endorse the remarriage of one partner (Lynda, our 'innocent' party), and 'forbid' the remarriage of the other. To be consistent, the church would have to tell both Ken and Lynda that they should remain single. Not least, because a remarriage for the 'innocent' party Lynda would mean that she is now in a sexual relationship with another man, thus giving a valid divorce to Ken, the remaining 'guilty' partner previously forbidden remarriage.

Such a black and white approach therefore has its own problems, and would probably be seen by many to be out of keeping with the message of the gospel, in that it suggests that there is another unforgivable sin apart from blaspheming the Holy Spirit (Mark 3:29)—it is that of having an invalid divorce.

But there are potential problems even if forgiveness *is* extended to Ken. I believe it would be difficult for the church leadership to conduct a marriage service for him and his new wife without, as suggested above (§9.9), causing offence to Lynda, Ken's divorced wife.

If Lynda indicated that she did not have a problem with Ken's remarriage within the fellowship, the oversight might still want further clarity from Ken on his understanding about marriage. However, Ken should not be forbidden marriage because he was the 'guilty party'—but his sinful behaviour is an issue to be addressed. If, in the end, the oversight decides Ken is not suitable husband material, while they could not forbid him marriage, they might choose not to conduct the service in their own fellowship, even though Lynda had indicated she would have accepted it.

If Ken remarries anyway and applies for membership at another church— what should the oversight's attitude of the new church be to such an application? Although Jesus said in Matthew 19:9, 'And I say to you: whoever divorces his wife, except for sexual immorality, and marries another, commits adultery'—as explained in §7.7, this 'adultery' relates to the covenantal faithlessness of an invalid divorce, not any remarriage.

The new church's oversight might choose to accept the new couple into membership on the basis that there is a difference between performing a marriage service for an invalidly divorced couple, and accepting such a couple into a fellowship. When a married couple join a church, it isn't usually thought appropriate to investigate their marital history.

When considering a remarriage when there has been an invalid divorce, or when a couple already remarried after an invalid divorce come to apply as members, it might be decided to have a short service of repentance, in public, or private. Any decisions about this would be up to the pastoral oversight of the fellowship and the couple involved.

9.11   Remarriage to a Previous Spouse

Charles and Susan

Are two believers that divorced many years ago and married other people. They are both now single and want to reinstate their first marriage.

The question here is: Does the Deuteronomy 24:1–4 teaching that forbids such a remarriage apply today? We have seen how Jeremiah uses this aspect of human marriage to illustrate a spiritual truth—Israel could not go back to God (§4.6). But Christ's death on the cross has circumvented this problem— all humanity can now freely go to Christ and participate in the marriage supper of the Lamb (§5.1). So I suggest that the Deuteronomy prohibition of remarriage to your original spouse does not belong to the church age either.

9.12   Divorcees in Church Leadership

It is not uncommon for a church fellowship to bar divorcees from a leadership role in the church. The qualifications for elders and deacons are listed in 1 Timothy 3:1–13 and Titus 1:5–9 —and there is no mention of divorce, except perhaps that an elder must be 'the husband of but one wife' (1 Timothy 3:2). This could be a reference to polygyny (the practice of taking more than one wife at a time), contemporary records showing that this was still Jewish practice in New Testament times. But 1 Timothy 5:9 says that a widow supported by the church must have been the 'wife of one husband.' And as there is no record of polyandry (the practice of taking more than one husband at a time) in either Israel or in the wider Ancient Near East, this brings into doubt a polygamy interpretation of either expression. Thus I suggest a valid interpretation is that husbands who are to be elders, and widows who are to be supported, should have been faithful to their spouses at the time of their marriage. To see that divorce *per se* should disqualify a person from leadership, demonstrates a misunderstanding of the concept. Divorce in and of itself is not sinful, rather it is a remedy for sinful behaviour—one that, as we have seen, both God the Father, and God the Son, exercised with Israel and Judah respectively (§4.5–§4.7; §5.6).

But what if a person was being considered for eldership and it was realised that before his conversion his abusive behaviour had resulted in a divorce? It might be thought that his pre-conversion behaviour should not count against him. Furthermore, the requirements for elders seem to emphasize the present marital status of the prospective elder, not his marital history.

In summary, if a candidate for a church leadership position is a divorcee, but they meet the qualifications that Paul lists in some detail in 1 Timothy 3 and Titus 1, there does not appear to be any scriptural reason to forbid them a leadership role. And what is more, as we have seen, in the Bible's marital imagery, the chief Shepherd (1 Peter 5:1–4) is portrayed as a divorcee, so it seems anomalous to deny a person an under-shepherd position on the grounds that they are divorced.

9.13   Summary

While the biblical principles of remarriage after divorce are clear, how to apply those principles within any particular fellowship might not be. Some might consider it hypocritical to suggest that in some cases within a local fellowship it might be wisest to ask a couple to marry elsewhere, on the basis that although the remarriage is legitimate, the church oversight was not happy about conducting the service. But sometimes, even though you would not personally commission an act, even though legitimate, you might accept a *fait accompli*.

Consider David and Bathsheba. David married Bathsheba after his adultery with her, and after he had ensured that Uriah had been killed in battle. We read that, 'the thing David had done displeased the Lord' (2 Samuel 11:26–27). Would Nathan, the prophet who condemned David, have conducted a marriage service for Bathsheba and David? I think this is unlikely. The Jewish (but not biblical) perspective seems to be that a man could not marry a woman he had been adulterous with.[61] But once presented with the marriage Nathan accepted the status quo. There was nothing in Old Testament teaching to forbid David's marriage. Nathan took the subsequent message from God that their second child (their first-born died) was loved by God. David named him Jedidiah, which means 'beloved of the LORD' (2 Samuel 12:24–25). God blessed this marriage with the birth of Solomon, who figures in the genealogy of Christ.

Chapter 10: Some Objections Considered

Some might consider that the understanding of the Bible's teaching on divorce and remarriage outlined in this book:

- **Makes divorce too easy**

It is true that a woman is allowed to initiate a divorce for reasons other than, but including, the sexual unfaithfulness of her husband, and that she is not forced, based on the clear teaching of Exodus 21, to stay with a husband against her will. But neither marriage, nor divorce, should be entered into lightly. The local church should play an active part in advising couples just what their marital obligations are, and only conduct a marriage ceremony when those obligations are fully understood and witnessed by the local congregation. Counselling should also occur before a divorce and everything possible done to keep the marriage together in a God honouring way.

- **Sets the cause of women's equality back**

It is true that women in the Bible's teaching do have different and more generous grounds for divorce than men. But that is God's way. The different grounds for divorce serve two purposes: for human marriage to reflect the relationship between Christ and his church, and to protect women.

- **Leaves men without the option for divorce from difficult or abusive wives**

But this understanding shares this position with the more traditional views of divorce. It is an outworking of the picture of Christ and the church. There is no easy answer to this problem, but it has been addressed in chapter 9.

- **Is teaching a doctrine based on the Lord's silence**

However, it is not the Bible's silence. Jesus did not specifically mention Exodus 21, but as has been seen the theme of that chapter is picked up in 1 Corinthians 7 (also Ephesians 5:25–30). What the more traditional views are in effect saying, is that Jesus *removes* the woman's grounds for divorce outlined in Exodus 21 by his silence on the subject. In New Testament exegesis, if a subject covered in the Old Testament is not mentioned, it is more usual to consider that the Bible's teaching on it has not changed.

- **Is teaching that an obscure verse in Exodus applies today**

The Exodus 21 teaching that a wife can expect to be provided for by her husband is the understanding demonstrated across the Ancient Near East for millennia before New Testament times. This is evidenced in every Jewish marriage contract that has been discovered from that era. Virtually all divorces initiated by women in Old Testament Israel were based on her husband's failure to meet his obligations for his wife's Exodus 21 entitlement.[62] The grounds for divorce in Exodus were the basis of the teaching of two prominent groups of Pharisees in New Testament times (the Hillelites and Shammaites), but they took opposing views on the interpretation of the 'any cause' grounds for a husband divorce in Deuteronomy 24. This is the question raised in Matthew 19 and Mark 10, and Jesus's answer endorsed the Shammaites' stricter interpretation of Deuteronomy 24. But he did not challenge their view that a wife had wider grounds for divorce based on the teaching of Exodus 21—or if Jesus did, the Bible does not record it.

- **Is teaching that the church has been wrong all these years**

The Roman Catholic teaching that marriage is a sacrament had developed over the centuries until it was formalised in 1563. The Reformers rejected that position, and adopted a divorce teaching that is widely held in the evangelical community today. They did not have access to the scholarship we now have, which has enabled us to see the context of the New Testament teaching more clearly.

As regards the traditional divorce views, they give rise to several theological, ethical, and pastoral problems, in that they:

- Teach that there is a radical discontinuity between the Old and New Testament, a discontinuity that is not seen in any other area.

- Teach that a wife's only ground for divorce is her husband's sexual unfaithfulness despite the fact the Bible never teaches that.

- Usually teach that divorce is only for 'adultery,' yet the Bible says divorce is for sexual immorality.

- Teach that remarriage is only for the 'innocent party,' despite the fact the Bible never teaches that.

- Give the impression there is another unforgivable sin, that of being a 'guilty' partner in marriage.

- Turn a blind eye to single people who have sexual intercourse outside marriage, yet penalise those that have married. Thus when a couple who are both single come forward for marriage, their previous private lives are not usually subject to investigation, but often, a once-married man or woman, subsequently divorced, is prohibited from marrying.

- Can tempt a couple into sin. A not uncommon situation is for a marriage to have irretrievably broken down, but there has been no infidelity. The couple is advised that there is no possibility of divorce unless there has been infidelity. This route can then become the easy way out of the marriage, especially if the church does offer forgiveness for a sinner, even for those involved in sexual sins.

- Are often pastorally 'unworkable.' The husband is an alcoholic, a wife beater—even a murderer, but because he has not committed a sexual sin the wife would be told in some churches that she cannot divorce him. If instead she murdered her husband, and was eventually released from prison, she would be more readily accepted in some churches than if she had divorced him.

- Give the impression that there are different rules for unbelievers. By teaching that the divorce rules are different in a 'mixed' marriage, the impression is given that God is less interested in the sexual morality of unbelievers.

- Bind a believer by the profession of another. A wife deserted by a 'believing' husband is told that she cannot remarry. Who is to know whether his profession is authentic? What if he had, unknown to his ex-wife, abandoned his profession of faith shortly after the divorce. The deserted wife would have had a life of singleness, bound by the false profession of her deserting husband. If the deserting partner had remarried, by definition the first marriage is repudiated, and in biblical terms the deserted partner would be free to marry. However, many of the traditional views would still hold that the deserted partner could not remarry.

- Lose the picture of Christ and the church. Perhaps this is the biggest drawback to the traditional views. By giving the husband and wife the same grounds for divorce, the picture of redemption embedded in marriage and divorce is lost.

Endnotes

[1] E. P. Sanders, *Jesus and Judaism* (London: SCM, 1985), 19; a literature review of material published in the last 100 years on the historical Jesus is contained in: James H. Charlesworth, *The Historical Jesus* (Nashville, TN: Abingdon, 2008), 6–12.

[2] C. H. Dodd, *According to the Scriptures* (London: Nisbet, 1952), 16.

[3] G. K. Beale, "Positive Answer to the Question: Did Jesus and His Followers Preach the Right Doctrine from the Wrong Texts?: An Examination of the Presuppositions of Jesus' and the Apostles' Exegetical Method," in *The Right Doctrine from the Wrong Texts?* ed. G. K. Beale (Grand Rapids, Mich.: Baker Books, 1994), 394, 398; similarly: Dodd, *According to the Scriptures*, 130.

[4] George B. Caird, *The Language and Imagery of the Bible* (London: Duckworth, 1980), 18, 144.

[5] Max Black, 'How Metaphors Work: A Reply to Donald Davidson,' in *On Metaphor*, ed. Sheldon Sacks (Chicago, IL: University of Chicago, 1978), 192.

[6] R. T. France, 'The Formula-Quotations of Matthew 2 and the Problem of Communication,' in Beale, *The Right Doctrine*, 133.

[7] Hays gives seven criteria to assess the probability of there being an allusion in any text of Scripture, and these are often referred to by other scholars: Richard B Hays, *Echoes of Scripture in the Letters of Paul* (New Haven, CT: Yale University Press, 1989), 29–32.

[8] Dorothy Sly, *Philo's Perception of Women* (BJS 209; Atlanta, GA: Scholars, 1990), 95; see an analysis in Colin Hamer, *Marital Imagery in the Bible: An Exploration of Genesis 2:24 and its Significance for the Understanding of New Testament Divorce and Remarriage Teaching* (London: Apostolos, 2015), §7.6.2.

[9] Richard B Hays, *The Conversion of the Imagination* (Grand Rapids, MI: Eerdmans, 2005), 43

[10] For an overview of the history of divorce and remarriage teaching in the Christian West see: David Instone-Brewer, *Divorce and Remarriage in the Bible: The Social and Literary Context* (Grand Rapids, MI: Eerdmans, 2002), 238–67; also: John Jr. Witte, *From Sacrament to Contract: Marriage, Religion, and Law in the Western Tradition*, 2nd ed. (Louisville, KY: Westminster John Knox, 2012), 1–112.

[11] Quentin Skinner, 'Meaning and Understanding in the History of Ideas,' *History and Theory* 8:1 (1969), 7, 40.

[12] Carol Meyers, *Discovering Eve: Ancient Israelite Women in Context* (New York, NY: Oxford University Press, 1988), 73.

[13] Bruce Kaye, '"One Flesh" and Marriage,' *Colloq* 2 (May 1990), 48–49; he cites: Genesis 29:14; 37:27; 2 Samuel 5:1; 19:12, 13; 1 Chronicles11:1; Nehemiah 5:5 and Job 2:5.

[14] Instone-Brewer, *Divorce and Remarriage*, 22.

[15] Gordon J. Wenham, *Genesis 1–15* (Nashville, TN: Word, 1987), 70.

[16] See analysis in: Colin Hamer, *Finding God's Will* (Eugene, Oreg.: Wipf and Stock, 2010), 35–38.

[17] Instone-Brewer, *Divorce and Remarriage*, 18.

[18] Raymond Westbrook, 'Adultery in Ancient Near Eastern Law,' *RB* 97 (1990), 577.

[19] John Witte points out that John Calvin in his later life saw that lessons could be learned from the Divine Marriage for human marriage: Witte, *From Sacrament to Contract*, 185–86.

[20] Instone-Brewer, *Divorce and Remarriage*, 34–35; also: Daniel I. Block, 'Marriage and Family in Ancient Israel,' in *Marriage and Family in the Biblical World*, ed. Ken M. Campbell (Downers Grove, IL: InterVarsity, 2003), 50–51.

[21] Dennis J. McCarthy, *Old Testament Covenant: A Survey of Current Opinions* (Stuttgart: Verlag Katholisches Bibelwerk, 1967; Repr. Oxford: Blackwell, 1972), 46–52, 58.

[22] McCarthy, *Old Testament Covenant*, 46–48, 55.

[23] Dennis J. McCarthy, 'Covenant in the Old Testament: The Present State of Enquiry,' *CBQ* 27 (1965), 235.

[24] William J. Dumbrell, *Covenant and Creation: An Old Testament Covenant Theology* (Milton Keynes: Paternoster, 2013), 50–51, 129, 259.

[25] Julie Galambush, *Jerusalem in the Book of Ezekiel: The City as Yahweh's Wife*, SBL Dissertation Series 130 (Atlanta, GA: Scholars, 1992), 147.

[26] Pseudepigrapha: *Joseph and Aseneth* 14:12–17.

[27] Josephus, *Jewish Antiquities* 9.288.

[28] Brant Pitre, *Jesus the Bridegroom: The Greatest Love Story Ever Told* (New York, NY: Crown, 2014), 69.

[29] Calum M. Carmichael, 'Marriage and the Samaritan Woman,' *NTS* 26 (1980), 337.

[30] A possible explanation to the anomaly is that the Baptist denied being in any literal sense Elijah, while the 'he is Elijah' of Matthew 11:14 is a metaphoric expression; Luke similarly links John the Baptist with the Malachi promise of a final messenger and cites Jesus as declaring Jerusalem's destruction: Luke 7:27; 13:34–35.

[31] George Lakoff and Mark Johnson, *Metaphors We Live By* (Chicago, IL: University of Chicago, 1980), 22.

[32] Westbrook, 'Adultery in Ancient Near Eastern Law,' 577.

[33] William R. G. Loader, *The New Testament on Sexuality* (Grand Rapids, MI: Eerdmans, 2012), 278. Loader elsewhere states when commenting on Genesis 2:24: 'The [LXX] translator used the word προσκολληθήσεται ("shall be joined/shall join") to translate the Qal, דָּבַק ("join to/stick to"). The range of meaning of both verbs is similar, including "cleave" and "stick". It need not be a sexual reference': William R. G. Loader, *The Septuagint, Sexuality, and the New Testament: Case Studies on the Impact of the LXX on Philo and the New Testament* (Grand Rapids, MI: Eerdmans, 2004), 41.

[34] G. K. Beale and Benjamin L. Gladd, *Hidden but Now Revealed* (Nottingham: Apollos, 2014), 178.

[35] Beale and Gladd, *Hidden but Now Revealed*, 181.

[36] Carmichael, 'Marriage,' 341–42.

[37] J. Paul Sampley, *And the Two Shall Become One Flesh: A Study of Traditions in Ephesians 5:21–33*, SNTSMS 16 (Cambridge: Cambridge University Press, 1971), 92–94, 161–62.

[38] Sampley, *And the Two*, 91; μυστήριον [mystery] appears seven times in Ephesians: Ephesians 1:9; 3:3, 4, 6, 9; 5:32; 6:19.

[39] Sampley, *And the Two*, 90–96, 162.

[40] Lynn R. Huber, *Like a Bride Adorned: Reading Metaphor in John's Apocalypse* (New York, NY: T&T Clark, 2007), 32.

[41] Catechism 1615: '[There is an] unequivocal insistence on the indissolubility of the marriage bond': Peter J. Kreeft, *Catholic Christianity: A Complete Catechism of Catholic Beliefs Based on the Catechism of the Catholic Church* (San Francisco, CA: Ignatius Press, 2001), 362.

[42] 'The Church of England agreed in 2002 that divorced people could remarry in church under certain circumstances. However, because the Church views marriage to be lifelong, there is no automatic right to do so and it is left to the discretion of the Priest': Church of England, 'As Someone Who is Divorced, Can I Marry in Church?' n.p. [cited 12 September 2015]. Online: <https://www.churchofengland.org/our-views/marriage,-family-and-sexuality-issues/divorce.aspx>. The impact of the Church of England teaching on the UK monarchy can be seen in the 1936 abdication of Edward VIII because of his decision to marry a divorcee, and the refusal of the Church to marry Prince Charles and the divorced Mrs Parker-Bowles while her ex-husband was still alive, hence their civil ceremony in 2005.

[43] See analysis in: Wayne H. House, ed., *Divorce and Remarriage: Four Christian Views* (Downers Grove, IL: InterVarsity, 1990); William A. Heth, 'Jesus on Divorce: How My Mind Was Changed,' *SBJT* 6.1 (Spring 2002), 4–12; Paul E. Engle and Mark L. Strauss, eds., *Remarriage after Divorce in Today's Church: 3 Views* (Grand Rapids, MI: Zondervan, 2006).

[44] The chart is from: David Instone-Brewer, 'Jesus' Old Testament Basis for Monogamy,' in *The Old Testament in the New Testament: Essays in Honour of J. L. North,* ed. Steve Moyise (Sheffield, England: Sheffield Academic, 2000), 92–93.

[45] Craig A. Blomberg, 'Marriage, Divorce, Remarriage, and Celibacy: An Exegesis of Matthew 19:3–12,' *TJ* 11NS (1990), 167–68.

[46] D. J. Moo, 'Jesus and the Authority of the Mosaic Law,' *JSNew Testament* 6, 20 (January 1984), 20.

[47] In the New American Bible (Revised Edition), which is the translation authorized by the U.S. Council of Catholic Bishops for use in the United States, Matthew 19:9 reads: 'I say to you, whoever divorces his wife (unless the marriage is unlawful [i.e. incestuous]) and marries another commits adultery.'

[48] Instone-Brewer, *Divorce and Remarriage*, 150.

[49] John Murray, *Divorce* (Phillipsburg, NJ: Presbyterian and Reformed, 1961), 100.

[50] Parker states: '"hard sayings" were hard from the beginning…. Passages which were the focus of contentious issues were particularly prone to change.' David M. Parker, 'The Early Traditions of Jesus' Sayings on Divorce Theology,' *Theology* 96 (1993), 378.

[51] Blomberg, 'Marriage,' 175, emphasis my own.

[52] Instone-Brewer states: 'There are no records of disputes among the rabbis about any of the grounds for divorce based on Exodus 21:10–11 except in matters of detail…. From at least the beginning of the first century it was recognized that the obligations of Exodus 21:10–11 could form the basis of a claim for divorce': Instone-Brewer, *Divorce and Remarriage,* 102.

[53] Canon 1086 states: 'A marriage between two persons, one of whom has been baptized in the Catholic Church or received into it and has not defected from it by a formal act and the other of whom is not baptized, is invalid': Vatican, 'Code of Canon Law,' <http://www.vatican.va/archive/ENG1104/_P3Y.HTM> [Accessed: 11/14/2014].

[54] Daube: 'An ancient law in Exodus [21:10] provides that … a man … may not "diminish" … [a first wife's] due. Paul no doubt uses the verb in the same sense when he admonishes married couples to fulfil their mutual obligations and not to "defraud" one another': David Daube, *The New Testament and Rabbinic Judaism* (Peabody, MA: Hendrickson, 1956), 365; similarly: Instone-Brewer, *Divorce and Remarriage,* 193; elsewhere Instone-Brewer comments: 'This reference to Exod 21:10–11 in 1 Corinthians 7:3–5 has not been widely recognised' but cites other publications that have: David Instone-Brewer, "1 Corinthians 7 in the Light of the Jewish Greek and Aramaic Marriage and Divorce Papyri," *TynBul* 52.2 (2001): 233 n. 29. The Exodus triad of obligation is also perhaps reflected in Eph 5:25–30.

[55] Blomberg, 'Marriage,' 188; also: Instone-Brewer, '1 Corinthians 7 in the Light of the Jewish Papyri,' 242.

[56] For example: *Mishnah Yebamot* 16:4.

[57] Ephesians 5:22–33; Colossians 3:19; Titus 2:4. For discussion of the concept of 'love' and other marital issues: Colin Hamer, *Being a Christian Husband: A Biblical Perspective* (Darlington: Evangelical Press, 2005).

[58] For a detailed analysis of the documents that demonstrate this see: Hamer, *Marital Imagery,* §8.3

[59] *Mishnah Ketubbot* 5:6

[60] Those who have expressed dismay to me about the suggestion that a wife has freedom to initiate a divorce on her own terms believe that it would lead to many divorces in the Christian community. But are we correct to have such a low view of Christian husbands? In a survey of married women in 2016, the results of which were broadcast on 10 October 2016, the BBC Radio 4 Woman's Hour programme found that 87% of women, if they had their time again, would marry the same man—and that is across all marriages, not marriages of Christian believers.
http://www.bbc.com/news/uk-37600771

[61] *Mishnah Yebamot* 2:8

[62] Instone-Brewer, *Divorce and Remarriage*, 20–33; 117–132, 150.